The Grounded Type of Sociological Theory

Igor Hanzel

The Grounded Type of Sociological Theory

Some Methodological Reflections

PETER LANG
EDITION

Bibliographic Information published by the Deutsche Nationalbibliothek
The Deutsche Nationalbibliothek lists this publication in the Deutsche Nationalbibliografie; detailed bibliographic data is available in the internet at http://dnb.d-nb.de.

Library of Congress Cataloging-in-Publication Data
Names: Hanzel, Igor, author.
Title: The grounded type of sociological theory:
some methodological reflection / Igor Hanzel.
Description: Frankfurt am Main; New York: Peter Lang, [2016] | Includes bibliographical references.
Identifiers: LCCN 2016042312 | ISBN 9783631672396
Subjects: LCSH: Grounded theory. | Sociology—Methodology.
Classification: LCC H61.24 .H36 2016 | DDC 300.1—dc23 LC record available at https://lccn.loc.gov/2016042312

This work was supported by the Slovak Research and Development Agency under the contract No. APVV-0149-12.

ISBN 978-3-631-67239-6 (Print)
E-ISBN 978-3-653-06797-2 (E-PDF)
E-ISBN 978-3-631-69717-7 (EPUB)
E-ISBN 978-3-631-69718-4 (MOBI)
DOI 10.3726/978-3-653-06797-2

© Peter Lang GmbH
Internationaler Verlag der Wissenschaften
Frankfurt am Main 2016
All rights reserved.
Peter Lang Edition is an Imprint of Peter Lang GmbH.

Peter Lang – Frankfurt am Main · Bern · Bruxelles · New York · Oxford · Warszawa · Wien

This publication has been peer reviewed.
www.peterlang.com

Acknowledgements

I am grateful to Professor Roman Ciapalo from Loras College, Dubuque, Iowa, to Dr. Miroslav Tížik from the Institute of Sociology of the Slovak Academy of Sciences, as well as to the referees who read the draft of this study and made numerous suggestions to improve it. Work on this study was supported by the Slovak Research and Development Agency under the contract number APVV-0149–12.

Abstract

The aim of this study is to analyze the methods used in the construction of the grounded type of sociological theory which is currently a widely used form of the qualitative direction in sociological research. It starts with an overview of three examples of qualitative research: *The social loss of a dying patient, Awareness of Dying*, and *Deviance disavowal*, the first two being classics in grounded theory. These examples then serve the purpose of delineating the principal characteristics of methods employed in the construction of the grounded type of theory. Next, the text explicates the characteristics of concepts, categories, and properties of categories employed in that type of theory, as well as the main steps involved in the construction of a grounded type of theory based on concepts, categories, and properties of categories. What follows is an explication, utilizing the approach of modern logic and methodology, of the nature of deduction, induction, and abduction, the last two – as is claimed very often by grounded theory representatives – being involved in the construction of the grounded type of theory. Finally, an attempt is made at a resolution of the dispute between the so-called qualitative and qualitative approaches to sociology.

Contents

"Those who can, do; those who cannot, teach; and those who have nothing to teach, become methodologists" (Lazarsfeld 1962, 757).

1. Introduction

The aim of this study is to analyze the methods used in the construction of the grounded type of sociological theory. This type is currently a widely used form of the qualitative direction in sociological research, the qualitative direction being understood as research where "mathematical techniques are eschewed or are of minimal use" (Strauss 1987, 2) and whose "findings [are] not arrived at by means of statistical procedures or other means of quantification" (Strauss – Corbin 1990, 17).[1]

I start with an overview of three examples of qualitative research: *The social loss of a dying patient* (Glaser – Strauss 1964), *Awareness of Dying* (Glaser – Strauss 1967), and *Deviance disavowal* (Davis 1961). These examples will serve the purpose of delineating the principal characteristics of methods employed in the construction of the grounded type of theory. The reason I start with examples of qualitative research is that the grounded type of sociological theory is in fact more than just a theory of social life, namely, a conceptualization of a research method.

Next, I explicate the characteristics of concepts, categories, and properties of categories employed in that type of theory. Then I analyze and reconstruct the main steps involved in the construction of a grounded type of theory as based on concepts, categories and properties of categories.

---

1   For a similar characteristic see (Glaser 1992, 11).

What follows is an explication, by employing the approach of modern logic and methodology, of the nature of deduction, induction, and abduction, the last two – as is claimed very often by grounded theory representatives – being involved in the construction of the grounded type of theory. Finally, I try to resolve the dispute between the so-called qualitative and qualitative approaches to sociology by dealing with Blumer's (1956) as well as Popper's (1957) approach to concepts quantity, magnitude and variable and show that neither of them distinguished these ideas properly. This will enable me to delineate the nature of qualitative direction in sociological research in a way which differs from Strauss' and at the same time provides its justification.

In order to prevent possible misunderstandings, I would like to emphasize that I do not deal in this study with social philosophy of symbolic interactionism, which provides the framework and basis for those three examples of qualitative research and for the grounded type of theory in general.[2]

As primary sources I use works which today are considered to be the standard presentations of research in the tradition of grounded type of sociological theory, in particular, (Glaser – Strauss 1965b), (Glaser – Strauss 1967), (Glaser 1978), (Strauss 1987), (Strauss – Corbin 1990) and (Charmaz 2006).

---

2   On this see for example (Strauss 1978), (Strauss 1984) and (Jeon 2004).

2. Three Studies

In this part I provide an overview of three examples of qualitative research.

2.1 The Social Loss of a Dying Patient

In a society a person is valued according to his/her different characteristics, such as age, ethnicity, education, race, family status, personality, accomplishments. A patient dying in a hospital embodies – in the eyes of a nurse – these characteristics, and the degree to which he/she embodies these characteristics is labeled by Glaser and Strauss as *social loss of a dying patient*. The degree of social loss of a dying patient determines the behavior of the nurse with respect to this patient: her sadness, stress, effort with which she takes care of the dying patient, etc.

When, for example, a society puts a high value on having lived a fulfilled life, then, the death of a child will be viewed by a nurse as a higher loss than that of an aged person who already had her share of life. In addition to age, other characteristics enter into the valuation of a patient's loss like education, social accomplishments, family status, and so forth. All these characteristics, once they have been acknowledged by the nurses, are labeled by Glaser and Strauss as the *patient's loss story*.

Another term that they introduce is that of *loss rationale*, which is useful in expressing a nurse's strategies in managing the stress and sadness due to the death of a patient she took care of. For example, the loss of a young man killed while driving in an illegal street race can be valued as relatively low by a nurse by means of a claim like "it was his own fault," while the burden caused by the death of a high loss patient, for example, a young mother with three small children, is eased by the claim that "it was a blessing she died; she was in terrible pain for several weeks."

2.2 Awareness of Dying

Drawing on the tradition of symbolic interactionism, Glaser and Strauss delineated the meaning of the term "awareness" in situations when "two interactants (whether persons or groups) … face the dual problem of being certain about their identity in the other's eyes and the other's identity" (1964a, 670).

The context in which awareness is given is then delineated as "the total combination of what each interactant in a situation knows about the identity of the other and his own identity in the eyes of the other" (1964a, 670). By "context" they understand (1964a, 670):

> a structural unit, not a property of one of the standard structural units such as group, organization, community, role, position, etc. By "context" we mean … a structural unit of an encompassing order larger than the other unit under focus: interaction. Thus, an awareness context surrounds and affects the interaction … *A more general definition of awareness context is the total combination of what specific people, groups, organization, communities or nations know what about a specific issue. Thus, this structural concept can be used for the study of virtually any problem entailing awareness at any structural level.*

Based on these delineations Glaser and Strauss focused on the interaction between, on the one hand, a dying patient, and, on the other hand, the hospital staff (nurses and doctors). To this interaction they assigned the following four types of awareness context for a detailed consideration.

Type 1. A *closed* awareness type of context which obtains when one of the interactants does not know either the other's identity or the other's understanding of his/her own identity.
Type 2. A *suspicion* type of awareness context obtains when one interactant suspects the true identity of the other or the other's understanding of his/her own identity, or both.
Type 3. A *pretense* type of awareness context obtains when both interactants are fully aware but pretend not to be.
Type 4. An *open* type of awareness context which obtains when each interactant is aware of the other's true identity and his/her own identity as understood by the other.

For research into those four types of awareness contexts Glaser and Strauss propose the following six directives to be followed:

Directive 1. Provide a description of the given type of awareness context.
Directive 2. Describe the structural conditions under which the awareness context exists.
Directive 3. Describe the consequent interaction.
Directive 4. Describe the changes that occasion transformation of context along with the structural conditions for the transformation.
Directive 5. Describe the tactics of interactants as they attempt to manage changes of the awareness context.
Directive 6. Describe some consequences of the initial awareness context, its transformation and associated interactions both for interactants and organization or institutions notably affected.

That typology and those directives were used by Glaser and Strauss in *Awareness of Dying* to answer the following questions pertaining to the interaction between a dying patient and the hospital staff (1965b, viii):

(1) How do the nurses and doctors manage themselves and their dying patient?
(2) What forms of social action arise while handling the dying patient?
(3) What are the social consequences for the staff and the hospital, as well as for the dying patient and his/her family?

Here, the term "awareness context" coined above turns into the term "awareness of dying" referring to "who in the dying situation, knows what about the probabilities of death for dying patient" (1965b, ix) or, stated otherwise, "[w]hat each interacting person knows of the patient's defined status, along with his recognition of the other's awareness of his own definition" (1965b, 10).

Accordingly, by employing this term, they aim at providing a unified conceptualization of "many events that otherwise might seem disconnected or paradoxical" (1965b, ix) and where "the efficacy of the scheme allows us to claim ... that discernible patterns of interaction occur predictably" (1965b, 8).

By employing the term "awareness of dying," the above stated three questions can be restated and broadened as follows (1965b, 8):

(1) What are the recurrent kinds of *interaction* between dying patient and hospital personnel?
(2) What kinds of tactics are used by the personnel dealing with the dying patient?
(3) Under what conditions of hospital organization do these kinds of interaction and these tactics occur?
(4) How do they affect the patient, his family, the staff and the hospital itself, all of whom are involved in the situations surrounding dying?

(5) How hospital personnel come to see the patient as due to die within some approximate time, and how they define their status and sometimes their "selves" in their relation with this patient.

The search for answers to these questions should be guided by six directives stated above, while some of them are transformed into the following ones (1965b, 11):

Directive 3*. Describe the consequent interaction, including various tactics and counter tactics.
Directive 4*. Describe the change of interaction from one type of awareness context to another.
Directive 5*. Describe the ways in which the interactants engineer changes of awareness contexts.
Directive 6*. Describe the various consequences of interaction for the interactants, for the hospital, and for further interactions.

Into the answers to those five questions enter, according to the authors, two criteria pertaining to *certainty of the death* and the *time of death*. The first criterion stands for "the degree to which the defining person (physician, nurse, or even the patient himself) is convinced that the patient will die" (1965b, 18). The second criterion pertains either to the time when the certain death will occur or when the certainty about the death will be resolved. By a combination of these criteria one obtains four possible types of situations labeled by Glaser and Strauss as *death expectation*. These types can be expressed as follows.

Table 1: Glaser's and Strauss' typology of death expectation

Death / Time of death	certain	uncertain
known	certain death at known time	uncertain death but a known time when the question will be resolved
unknown	certain death at unknown time	uncertain death at unknown time when the question will be resolved

Utilizing the typology given in this table, they can conceptualize the varying effects of death expectation on the interaction between the dying patient and the hospital staff in the above mentioned types of awareness context.

The *closed* awareness type of context was identified by Glaser and Strauss as given in hospitals in the USA in the early 1960s when patients frequently did not recognize the signs of his/her impending death even when the personnel had already this information.

The structural conditions contributing to the existence and maintenance of that type of awareness context are as follows (1965b, 30–32):

(1) Most patients are not especially experienced at recognizing the signs of impending death.
(2) US physicians ordinarily do not tell the patients outright that death is probable or inevitable.
(3) Families guard the secret of impending death.
(4) The hospital is organized in such a way and the hospital personnel behave in such a way that information about the patient is hidden from the latter.

(5) The patient has no allies who would reveal or help him/her to discover the personnel's knowledge of impending death.

As an aid to understanding the continuation and maintenance of the closed type of awareness context, Glaser and Strauss coin two additional terms, namely, *fictional biography* and *assessment management*. The first expresses the attempt of the personnel to construct a fictional biography of the patient for this patient in order to sustain his/her belief that he/she will recuperate. The second term refers to the attempt on the part of the personnel to manage the patient's assessment of events pertaining to his/her belief into the biography constructed by the personnel.

One of the *consequences* of the closed type of awareness context dealt with by Glaser and Strauss is that the patient, so as he/she believes in the biography presented to him/her by the personnel, becomes extremely cooperative with the personnel, believing that a faithful follow up of their orders will speed up recovery and an early release from the hospital.

Some of the above given conditions of continuation and maintenance of the closed type of awareness context can change and in such a case the patient moves either to suspicion or full awareness of the impending death.

For the *suspicion* type of awareness context holds that the patient who suspects that he/she is dying tries to verify this suspicion while others, who recognize that he suspects, simultaneously make attempts to negate his/her suspicion. Here the patient does not know for sure but only suspects with a varying degree of certainty that the personnel believe him/her to be dying.

The existence of the personnel's recognition of the patient's suspicion is crucial for the presence of this type of awareness context. If it is not given then, in Glaser's and Strauss' typology of awareness contexts, this type is not given; instead two other types are classified as belonging to the closed type. One is given when the patient is suspicious, but the hospital staff does not recognize this suspicion. Another is given when the staff wonders but is not sure whether the patient does suspect the impending death. Or they may wonder if he/she really knows about the impending death but does not reveal his/her knowledge.

In the mode of interaction given in the suspicion type of awareness context, contrary to the closed type, a contest for the control of the interaction takes place between the patient and the personnel. This context is viewed as one of the structural conditions of this type of awareness context as reconstructed by Glaser and Strauss; into the set of these conditions they include also the patient's inquiry and tactics as well as staff's tactics and counter tactics.

Then, again following the above given directives, they delineate the consequences of the suspicion type of awareness context as well as the directions into which can change. Following these directives, they then conceptually treat also the *pretense* and *open* types of awareness context (1965b, 64–106).

2.3 Deviance Disavowal

The paper (Davis 1961) deals with social interactions, in which one of the interactants is viewed by the other interactant as deviant, but the former refuses to concur with the verdict of the latter.

The type of deviance which according to Davis can be ascribed in the course of interaction ranges from race, via sexual orientation up to a visible physical handicap; the latter being the focus of that paper. The latter scrutinizes interactions with deviance ascription and refusal taking place and which are 1) face-to-face; 2) prolonged enough to permit more than a fleeting glimpse or exchange, but not so prolonged that close familiarity ensues; 3) intimate to the extent that the interactants must pay more than perfunctory attention to one another, but not so intimate that the customary graces can be dispensed with; and 4) ritualized to the extent that all know what to be expected, but not so ritualized as to preclude spontaneity and a slightly novel turn of events.

The paper is based on interviews with a small number of visibly (orthopedically, or blind, or facially disfigured) handicapped persons, and enquires into their handling of imputations by their non-handicapped counterparts that they are "not normal" in the sense of deviating from everyone else. These imputations manifest themselves in a "stickiness" of interactions and in the embarrassment of the "normal" interactant conveying the message that he/she is finding it difficult to relate to the handicapped when compared to any other "normal" interactant and can be read from slips of tongue, revealing gestures and inadvertent remarks.

The interaction in which one of the interactants has a visible handicap is burdened by a threat which can be at least fourfold. First, the visible handicap can become an exclusive focus of interaction. Second, the handicap can inundate the expressive dimension of interaction so that the outward expressions deemed most salient for the given occasion of interaction (e.g., pleasure, warm interest) can become dissonant with emotions expressing the "normal" interactant's inner states. Third, it can get into discordance with other attributes of the handicapped. Fourth, the handicap can hamper a joint activity of the "normal" interactant and visibly handicapped one, for example, when the former doubts if the latter can participate at all in certain types of activities, for example, attending a concert, visiting a theater or to be included in a kind of sporting event.

Based on that delineation of the fourfold threat, the central question posed in (Davis 1961) is "how socially adept handicapped persons cope with it so as to either keep it at bay, dissipate it or lessen its impact upon the interaction" (1961, 125). The answer stands for a delineation of stages through which interaction of a visibly handicapped with non-handicapped typically passes in a type of society which is usually labeled as "Western." Here are three of these stages (1961, 125–131).

Stage 1. Fictional acceptance in the sense that the visibly handicapped is customarily accorded the surface acceptance that democratic manners guarantee to all.

Stage 2. "Breaking through" in the sense of moving beyond the fictional acceptance and which takes place in a normalization process where the handicapped projects images and attitudes of self so that the non-handicapped interactant can understand the role in the interaction of the handicapped interactant as different from that associated with the visible handicap.

Stage 3. Institutionalization of the normalized relationship, in the sense that interaction is sustained in the face of many small amendments and qualifications. For example a wheel-chaired person has to develop together with the non-handicapped a set of routines helping them together to master a descent from stairs or entering a city bus.

3. Construction of a Grounded Type of Theory

In this part I explicate the steps employed in the construction of the grounded type of theory as well as the characteristics of concepts, categories, and properties of categories employed in this construction.

In (Glaser – Strauss 1967) the authors gave a characterization of the methods employed in the generation of the grounded type of theory. The starting point of this characterization is the reflection on the situation they actually faced in the mid-1960s in the literature on methods applied in sociology which they viewed as "concerned with how accurate facts can be obtained and how theory can thereby be more rigorously tested" (Glaser – Strauss 1967, 1). Their own aim, as an alternative to this, is to "address ... to the equally important enterprise of *how the discovery of theory from data can ... be furthered*. We believe that the discovery of theory from data—which we call *grounded theory*—is a major task confronting sociology today" (1967, 1).[3]

So, the term "grounded theory" refers according to Glaser and Strauss not only to a product of research, but also to a process of "discovery of theory from data systematically obtained from social research ... Our basic position is that generating grounded theory is a way of arriving at theory suited to its supposed uses" (1967, 2–3).

---

3   On this see also (Charmaz 1983). For a comparison of grounded type of sociological theory with alternative types see (John 1980).

Among the uses of grounded theory they list the following (1967, 3):

(1) Prediction and explanation of behavior.
(2) Enhancement of theoretical advance in sociology,
(3) Practical applications—prediction and explanation should be able to give the practitioner understanding and some control of situations.

The generation of grounded theory from data can also be viewed as a "careful method of idea manufacturing" (Glaser 1978, 7) in the sense of a "meaning making activity" (Glaser 1998, 140), and where the forms this meaning acquire are related to the terms like, for example, "social loss of a patient" and "loss rationale" mentioned above. These meanings are classified in the grounded type of sociological theory as *categories* and/or *properties of a category*.

3.1 Indices, concepts, categories and properties of categories

The above mentioned primary orientation of the grounded type of sociological theory to theory generation is realized as a movement from data to concepts; "A concept may be generated from one fact, which then becomes merely a universe of many possible diverse indicators for, or data on, the concept" (Glaser – Strauss 1967, 23).

So, for example, the concept related to the caring for a dying patient in a hospital is that of *social loss of a dying patient*. This concept "can be generated from either the observation that VIP's receive special care on intensive care units or that lower-class Negroes often are neglected on city hospital emergency wards" (1967, 24). Indicators (incidents in the data under analysis – Holton 2007, 244) play a central role in the generation of a grounded type of theory because it is "based on a *concept-indicator model*, which directs the conceptual coding of a set of empirical indicators. This model provides the essential link between data and concept, which results in a theory generated from data" (Glaser 1978, 62).

This direction of movement from indicators, based on their mutual comparisons, to concepts can be expressed as follows (1978, 62):

Fig. 1: The concept-indicator model

Concept

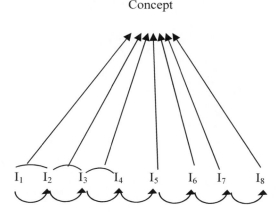

I_1 I_2 I_3 I_4 I_5 I_6 I_7 I_8

So, for example, by dealing with the apparent and learned facts as acquired by a nurse about the previous life of a dying patient she is taking care of, these facts can serve the sociologist for the purpose of the generation of the concept of social loss acquired by the nurse. The figure expressing the generation of this concept can be expressed as follows (1978, 63).

*Fig. 2: The generation of the category of social loss from its
apparent and learned indicators*

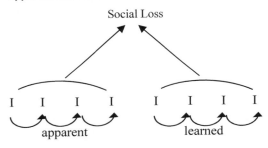

The entities labeled in the sociological tradition of grounded
theory as "concepts" are further differentiated into *conceptual categories*, or *categories*, for short, and *properties of
categories*. For example, the concept of *social loss of a dying
patient* is viewed as a category and the concept of *loss rationale* is viewed as a conceptual aspect or element (property) of
that category.

Stated in a more general way, in the tradition of the
grounded theory a category is viewed as an independent,
conceptual element of a grounded type of theory which is
of a higher order (level) of abstraction compared to that of
a property of this category (Kelle 1994, 290; Glaser 1998,
135; Strauss and Corbin 1990, 61).[4]

3.2 Steps in the construction of a grounded type of
sociological theory

Data, indicators, categories and properties of categories are
interrelated in the process of theory construction. The central

---

4 On this see also (Dey 1999, 49–63).

steps in this construction are *data collection*, *coding* and the *employment of codes* (substantive and theoretical), of *coding families*, *coding paradigms* and *constant comparison* by means of *theoretical sampling* which should ultimately yield a theory as the "end"-product indicated by reaching the state of the so-called "theoretical saturation."

Data collection in a substantive area (e.g., care for a dying patient in a hospital) usually starts either by a confused state of tentatively noting everything the sociologist sees or by focusing initially on a generally delineated problem in a substantive area under investigation (Glaser – Strauss 1965a, 5–6; Glaser 1978, 44). The "first" data pertain to the investigated entities (situations, persons, documents, etc.) which are chosen in a research process with an explorative nature (Truschkatt – Kaiser-Belz – Reinartz 2007).

What enters into the data collection as a pregiven conceptual presupposition is a general sociological perspective. In the case of the grounded type of sociological theory it is symbolic interactionism; what should not in any way enter into that collection is a pregiven system of concepts and hypotheses pertaining directly to the substantive area under investigation.

Coding is understood in the tradition of grounded theory as "operations by which data are broken down, conceptualized, and put back together in new ways" (Strauss – Corbin 1990, 57). These operations stand for attaching "labels to segments of data that depict what each segment is about. Coding distills data, sorts them, and gives us a handle for making comparisons with other segments of data … By making and coding numerous comparisons, our analytic grasp of the data begins to take form" (Charmaz 2006, 3).

To be more specific, the coding of data stands for assigning codes to certain passages of data given to the sociologist in the form of written material (e.g., transcripts of interviews and field notes). Charmaz gives the following illustration of the initial coding operations performed on statements made by chronically ill persons, and where the coding targets persons' experience of time and self (1983, 116):

Table 2: *Examples of initial coding of interview statements into codes (Charmaz 1983, 116)*

Interview statements coded into ——————➤ codes	
A 29 year old *with renal failure was discussing his high school years, and events that occurred long before he was diagnosed.* ... I knew I was different. I caught colds very easily and my resistance was very low, and so I knew that generally speaking my health was not as good as everybody else's, but I tried to do all the things that everybody else was doing.	Self-perception Awareness of difference Identifying self through ill health Comparing health to others'
A 54 year old *woman who had had cancer and currently had a crippling autoimmune disease was explaining her view on why she had had a recurrence of cancer.* When I look back on my second bout of cancer, I was not feeling good about myself and the whole struggle of the last three years put me into X (cancer institute) to get me to feel better about myself.	Self in retrospect Self-esteem Outcome of timed struggle Improving self-esteem as treatment goal

In the tradition of grounded theory several different views on the *types and sequences of coding procedures* were developed. Here I mention three such views.

According to *Glaser*, there exist two types of coding: *substantive* coding enabling to "conceptualize the empirical substance of the area of research" (1978, 55) and *theoretical* coding enabling to "conceptualize how the substantive codes may relate to each other as hypotheses to be integrated into the theory" (1978, 55).

In Glaser's typology substantive coding's starting point is *open* coding which then transforms into *selective* coding. The former stands for "coding the data in every way possible … 'running the data open'. The analyst codes for as many categories possible that might fit … It begins with the fracturing of data into analytic pieces, Open coding … gets one 'out of his data'" (1978, 56).

There exists according to him six rules governing open coding (1978, 57–58).

Rule 1. Ask the following questions of the data: "What is this data a study of?"; "What category or property of category, of what part of the emerging theory, does this incident indicate?"; "What is actually happening in the data?"; "What is the basic social psychological process or social structural process?"

Rule 2. Analyze the data line by line, constantly coding each sentence.

Rule 3. As an analyst, make your own coding; you obtain codes you did not have before categories emerged.

Rule 4. Interrupt coding to write memos about the ideas about the codes.

Rule 5. In the course of coding you should stay within the confines of the substantive area.

Rule 6. Do not assume the analytic relevance of any variable (e.g., age, sex, social class, race, skin color, etc.) until it emerges as relevant.

In *selective coding* the emerging theory is delimited to a central, *core category* enabling to focus the ongoing research on the central issues (e.g., the basic social process), while assigning to the remaining categories the status of subordinated categories. This then, in turn, leads to a focusing of "coding to only those variables that relate to the core variable in sufficiently significant ways to be used in a parsimonious theory ... The analyst looks for the conditions and consequences that ... relate to the core process. His analysis is guided by the core variable" (Glaser 1978, 61).

Theoretical coding stands, according to Glaser, for a higher-order unification of substantive codes into theoretical codes. A vital role is played here by the so-called coding families which I will list further below.

Strauss differentiates between three stages of coding: open, axial and selective (Strauss – Corbin 1990, 62–129).

In *open* coding, data are broken down and compared so that their similarities and differences between incidents are revealed. This enables one to identify in them a similar phenomenon which is then conceptualized as a category to be further developed in terms of its properties.

In *axial* coding, the data – after being broken down – are put together from the point of view of general categories which are interconnected by employing a coding paradigm. The latter's elements are quite similar to the elements of Glaser's coding families, I will list them both below.

In *selective* coding a category is chosen as the core one, around which are centered and with which are integrated other categories. The rules to be followed here are as follows (1990, 116–118)

Rule 1. Explain the story line in the sense of providing a conceptualized narrative of the central phenomenon of the substantive area under investigation.

Rule 2. Relate the subsidiary categories to the core category by means of the coding paradigm.

Rule 3. Relate the categories at the dimensional level in the sense of assigning to them continua along which they vary.

Rule 4. Validate these relationships against data.

Rule 5. Fill in categories that may need further refinement and development.

Charmaz viewed the coding process as involving the following steps (2006, 43–70).

Initial coding, taking its course either word by word, or line by line, or incident by incident, clarifies what the data is a study of, what does this data suggest (pronounce), from whose point of view, what theoretical category does the specific datum indicate.

Focused coding, here the most significant codes are used to sift through large amounts of data so as to categorize them incisively and completely.

She also shares Strauss' views on axial coding as well as Glaser's views on theoretical coding. For a better understanding of her views on coding I reproduce her examples on focused coding as follows (1983, 119):

Table 3: *Examples of focused coding of interview statements into codes (Charmaz 1983, 119)*

Interview statement coded into ──────► codes	
A woman with intensive experience in undergoing bureaucratic evaluations responded to my questions about how she felt about being scrutinized. … All I can do is dissolve in tears – there's nothing I can do. I just get *immobilized* – you just sort of reach a point, you can't improve, can't remedy the situation, and you're told you aren't in the right category for getting services you need and can't get for yourself. It makes me madder and madder at myself for being in the situation in the first place.	Relation of interactional sources of self-pity and self-blame
The following observation was made during an interview with a retired college professor and his wife, both of whom had chronic illnesses. … I asked "Did you keep up with professional work after you retired?" He said "I used to teach extension courses but with the budget and that governor, there isn't any money for extension courses." She [his wife] cut in [to me], "Andrei used to be an extremely successful speaker; partly his enthusiasm, partly his articulateness, but with the speech problem, he can't do it … [He, slowly and painfully] "The schools don't have any money … I can't speak well."	Negative identifying moment

Let me now turn to the conceptual input into the process of coding. This input is labeled by Glaser under the caption "coding families" and by Strauss under "coding paradigm." The former can be summarized as follows (Glaser 1978, 73–80):[5]

Table 4: *Glaser's coding families in Theoretical Sensitivity of 1978*

Family-name	Subject-matter	Elements
Six C's	Causal models	Causes, contexts, contingencies, consequences, covariance, and conditions
Process	Process-models	Stages, phases, progressions
Degree	Degree of attributes	Limit, range, intensity, etc.
Dimension	Patterns of connections	Elements, divisions, properties, etc.
Types	Types	Type, form, kinds, styles, etc.
Strategy	Strategies of action	Strategies, tactics, mechanisms, etc.
Interaction	Mutual interactions	Mutual effects, reciprocity, mutual trajectory, etc.
Identity-Self	Concepts of the self	Self-image, self-concept, self-worth, etc.
Cutting Point	Cutting points	Boundary, critical juncture, turning point, etc.
Means-Goal	Concepts of purposeful action	End, purpose, goal, etc.

---

5 Here I draw also on (Mey – Mruck 2007) and (Dey 1999). For an enlargement of the list of coding families by Glaser, see his (1998, 170–175) and (2005, 22–29).

Family-name	Subject-matter	Elements
Cultural	Cultural phenomena	Norms, values, beliefs, etc.
Consensus	Social consensus	Clusters, agreements, contracts, etc.
Mainline	Social integration	Social control, recruitment, socialization, etc.
Theoretical	Concepts for generating, criticizing and judging theory	Parsimony, scope, integration, etc.
Ordering or Elaborating	Ordering of data, concepts and categories	Structural, temporal, conceptual
Unit	Units of social life	Collective, group, nation, etc.
Reading	Way of Coding	Concepts, problems and hypotheses
Models	Modeling of theory	Linear, spatial, etc.

Strauss' coding paradigm involves the following codes (Strauss – Corbin 1990, 96–97):

Code 1. *Causal conditions* in the sense of events, incidents, happenings that lead to the occurrence or development of a phenomenon.

Code 2. *Phenomenon* in the sense of the central idea, event, happening, incident about which a set of actions or interactions are directed at managing, handling, or to which the set of actions is related.

Code 3. *Context* in the sense of the specific set of properties that pertain to a phenomenon; that is, the locations of events or incidents pertaining to a phenomenon along a dimensional range. It represents the particular set of conditions within which the action/interactional strategies are taken.

Code 4. *Intervening conditions* in the sense of structural conditions bearing on action/interactional strategies pertaining to a phenomenon. They facilitate or constrain the strategies taken within a specific context.

Code 5. *Action/Interaction* in the sense of strategies devised to manage, handle, carry out, and respond to a phenomenon under a specific set of perceived conditions.

Code 6. *Consequences* in the sense of outcomes of action and interaction.

Let me now turn to *constant comparison, theoretical sampling* and *theoretical saturation.*

As shown above, the starting point for the generation of particular categories was the mutual comparison of incidents picked up from samples belonging to a group of entities (events, persons, etc.) and where this group was known *before* the respective category was generated. So, for example, the category *social loss of a dying patient* emerged from a comparison of nurses' reaction to the looming death of their patients.

Thus, the rule being here at work is as follows: *While coding an incident for a category, compare the incident with previous incidents in the same sample from a group in order to establish an underlying uniformity* (Holton 2007, 250).[6] According to Glaser (1998, 25):

> When comparing incident to incident when coding his field notes, the researcher begins to see a pattern and a concept emerges that fits it. A category or its property has emerged. The researcher keeps asking "what category does this incident indicate?" or "what property of what category does this in-

---

6 This formulation differs from the formulation of this rule in (Glaser – Strauss 1967, 106).

cident indicate?" The concept emerges as the constant comparative process proceeds. In continuously comparing further incidents to the concept, the researcher starts seeing the same thing over and over again in different ways.

Subsequently, the generated categories are compared to incidents given in samples drawn from groups different from that group for which the category was initially generated. These new samples as well as the new groups of entities are chosen in the light of the already emerged category, that is, the search for them and their choice is now already *category-driven*. This choice of new samples is standardly labeled in the tradition of grounded theory as *theoretical sampling*.[7] The latter "in conjunction with constant comparison … is the process whereby the researcher decides what data to collect next and where to find them in order to continue to develop the theory as it emerges. As such, the process of data collection is controlled by the emerging theory" (Holton 2007, 25).[8] That is, the return to data collection is now already theory driven.

So "[b]eyond the decisions concerning the initial collection of data, further collection cannot be planned in advance of the emerging theory … The emerging theory points to the next steps—the sociologist does not know them until he is guided by the emerging gaps in his theory and by research questions suggested by previous answers" (1967, 47). For example, when dealing with the awareness of dying in a hospital, the ward from which the incidents of patient-staff interaction were chosen was such, where patients' awareness had to be taken into account by the staff. A shift to another ward could then be performed, where patients' awareness

---

7 For strategies involved in theoretical sampling see (Morse 1991).
8 On this see also (Glaser – Strauss 1967, 45).

need not be taken into account, as it is, for example in an emergency ward.[9]

The reasons for theoretical sampling, according to Glaser and Strauss (1967, 55), are two-fold.

First, by choosing different groups and by means of their comparison, one can control the scale of generality of the emerging theory in the sense of the level of conceptualization and population scope.

Second, by choosing different groups and by means of their comparison, one can minimize and maximize the differences and similarities of data and where both are crucial for the gradual emergence of theory.

The basic consequences of maximizing and minimizing the differences between the groups targeted by the grounded type of theory can be expressed as follows (Glaser – Strauss 1967, 88):

Table 5: *Basic consequences of minimizing and maximizing differences between groups for the grounded type of theory*

Data / Differences in groups	similar	diverse
minimized	Minimal differences between data lead to: (1) verifying the usefulness of an already generated category; (2) generating basic properties of a category; (3) establishing a set of conditions for a degree of a category.	Spotting fundamental differences under which category and hypotheses vary

---

9   On this see Chapter 7 in (Glaser – Strauss 1967).

Data Differences in groups	similar	diverse
maximized	Spotting fundamental uniformities of greatest scope	Maximum diversity in data forces: (1) dense development of properties of category; (2) integrating categories and properties; (3) delimiting scope of theory

The most important criterion for choosing groups for mutual comparison is that of *theoretical relevance* in a twofold sense. First, the comparison should enable one to move from one level of theory to another in the sense of movement from data to categories, to the latter's properties as well as to their dimensions, and to the level where the relations between categories are stated. Second, it should enable one to increase the universality of the theory in the sense of its applicability to a wide range of groups (Glaser – Strauss 1967, 49–52).

The state where the sociologist should stop sampling is reached when no additional sampling from groups yield data enabling the introduction of a new category, or new properties of a category, or new relations between categories. This state is labeled in the tradition of grounded theory as *theoretical saturation*.[10]

The emergence of the state of saturation in the course of theory generation depends on two factors: sociologist's state of knowledge of data and the state of affairs in the substan-

---

10 For details on theoretical saturation see (Morse 1995).

tive area, and where both these factors display their own specific dynamics.

As to the dynamics of knowledge, the sociologist never knows in advance if he/she will face new data which cannot be conceptualized by means of the already emerged network of categories and their properties. Once they cannot be, then this network has to be modified. So, for example, after Glaser and Strauss found out that the age of a dying patient is one of crucial factors for establishing the social loss of patient, they came across a case where the dying of an 85-year-old woman was viewed by the personnel as a great social loss. In order to integrate this case into their network of categories, they coined the additional property "wonderful personality" in order to account for a factor which outweighed the factor of age in the establishment of the social loss by the personnel (1967, 111).

The dynamics of the state of affairs in the substantive area under investigation can lead to a complete invalidation of a given network of categories and properties. So, for example, the starting point of *Awareness of Dying* was the situation in the mid-1960s when most people in the US were dying in hospitals. We can imagine a change of this situation so that most people would die at home; then the network of categories developed in this classic in the tradition of grounded theory could not be applied to this new situation.

3.3 A method of theory development

An example of sampling, in the sense of data collection driven by an emerging theory, is Strauss' article (1970) which draws on Davis' article dealt with above.

In order to understand the method of theory development proposed by Strauss, let me first list the central characteristics of the substantive area of Davis' article. It is the *interac-*

39

tion between persons 1) which takes place for the *first* time; 2) *face-to-face*; 3) between *two* persons; 4) *one* of which is handicapped while the *other* not; 5) this handicap is *visible* to the non-handicapped; 6) it occurs in *"sociable" situations* in the sense that it is neither impersonal (not encompassing, for example, ritualized interaction) nor intimate; 7) where the handicapped *attempts to minimize* the handicap; 8) where the handicapped *controls* the interaction, while the non-handicapped accepts this; 9) it is *strained* in the sense that the handicapped tries to intrude into it; and 10) where *the handicapped is already experienced in managing strained interactions*.

By listing these ten characteristics, it is possible to consider the directions in which the categories given in (Davis 1961) can be further developed. The starting point for such a development is a set of hypothetically considered characteristics of interactions which are opposed to those listed above. Interaction 1*) does *not* takes place for the first time; 2*) it is not *face-to-face* (but takes place, e.g., by phone) 3*) is between *more than two* persons; 4*) is between *more than one handicapped* and/or *more than one non-handicapped*; 5*) the handicap is *not visible* to the non-handicapped; 6*) occurs in *"non-sociable" situation* in the sense that it is either impersonal (encompassing, e.g., ritualized interaction) or intimate; 7*) the handicapped *does not try to minimize* the handicap; 8*) the non-handicapped *controls* the interaction, while the handicapped *accepts* this; 9*) is *not strained* in the sense that the handicapped does not try to intrude into it; and 10*) *the handicapped is not experienced in managing strained interactions*.

By opposing characteristics 1*) through 10*) to characteristics 1) to 10), it is possible to start developing a network of categories, which draws on Davis' network. The central point here is the generation of new categories which is of a hypothetical nature and where these categories should fit interactions fulfilling the conditions 1*) through 10*).

For example, in the case of the interaction of handicapped person with a non-handicapped person, where the handicap is not visible to the latter, the category introduced as a hypothesis is that of *secrecy*. Theoretical sampling in the sense of a category-driven search for relevant data would then consist in a search for persons who try to keep the secret of their handicap for themselves, for example, women after a mastectomy, who then could be subjected to a series of interviews.

4. Metareflections

In this part I address the methodological aspects of the above given characteristics of the grounded type of theory. Its principal features can be expressed by the following catch-phrases: *cyclical nature of theory construction, a continuous increase of conceptual density in the course of theory construction,* and *unit busting in the course of theory construction.*

After dealing with these features, I will turn to their relations to *deduction, induction,* and *abduction,* where the last two – as is usually claimed in the tradition of grounded theory – should play a central role in the course of inference of categories and of properties of categories from data.

4.1 Research cycles, increase of conceptual density and unit busting

The specific feature of the process of theory construction in the tradition of grounded theory is that this construction is of a *bi-directional* nature: going from data to categories and their properties and from the categories and their properties, via theoretical sampling, "back" to data. So, for example, in (Charmaz 2006, 101) one can read with respect to theoretical sampling the following:

> Theoretical sampling is purposeful sampling but it's purposeful sampling according to categories that one develops from one's analysis ... they're based on theoretical concerns ... Theoretical sampling really makes grounded theory special and is the major strength of grounded theory *because* theoretical sampling allows you to tighten what I call the corkscrew of the hermeneutic spiral so that you end up with a theory that perfectly matches your data.

Glaser expressed this as follows: "The stages of grounded theory research may very well cycle in circles" (1998, 15). The cyclical-processual nature of research in that tradition is represented by Charmaz in the following figure (2006, 11):[11]

Fig. 3: *Cyclical process of construction of grounded type of theory*

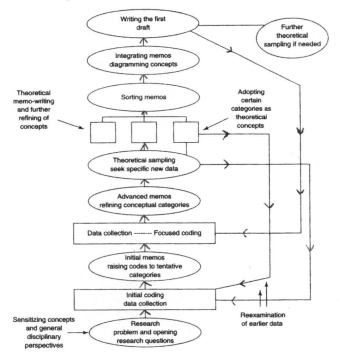

---

11 I added arrows to the lines in Charmaz's original figure.

What takes place in the course of the cyclically proceeding research is a gradual construction of a network of categories related to both their properties and other categories. This thus means that the research process as accomplished in the tradition of grounded theory yields a gradually increased *conceptual density*. For example, Strauss comments his method of developing the network of categories proposed in (Davis 1961) as follows (1970, 50; italics are mine – I.H.)

> If we pursue this analysis, we can eventually develop testable hypotheses about each class of handicapped person as these people interact in sociable or other situations with normal or other handicapped people. The hypotheses are designed ... to add *density of conceptual detail to our evolving theory*.

Once shifting from the research of visibly handicapped to that of non-visibly handicapped and by sampling women after mastectomy, the researcher faces questions which he/she tries to answer by collecting new data via interviews. These questions being, for example: "Is the loss [of a breast] more likely to be a dread and guarded secret for unmarried young women than for young mothers? For young mothers than for elderly mothers?" (1970, 50). When these questions are posed, then the sociologist can pursue the research in a different direction; "He can ... pursue the case of the patient operated on for a mastectomy, turning her around as if she were a complexly cut diamond and examining her many facets. How do these women act in various types of nonsociable interaction? ... How do they perform in the successive episodes of social interaction, rather than in just the first episode?" (1970, 51).

Accordingly, the general methodological moral from questions of this type is as follows: "As the theorist answers these questions (in imagination or later with data), he builds hypotheses of varying scope and different degrees of abstraction … Thus he continues to build conceptual density into his theory" (1970, 51).

Yet another feature of theory construction in the tradition of grounded theory is that the *universe of entities for which the theory is stated gradually changes in the course of this construction*.[12]

This change takes place in the course of theoretical sampling enabling a generalization of the theory by changing its scope. The latter was labeled by Glaser as unit busting and understood as follows (1998, 160):

> Theoretical sampling is unit busting in two ways. Grounded theory generalizes to a conceptual unit which is the core category. It readily takes sampling outside the boundaries of the unit it may have begun with. Researchers typically like to start a study in a unit where a clear instant of their interest is located … The tendency is to start generating a theory … and looking elsewhere beyond the unit to generate more properties of [the category] … By constantly coding and analyzing the original unit is soon left behind as too descriptive as the researcher goes conceptual … By theoretical sampling the theory has left time and place and expanded well beyond the limited properties of the original unit. Obviously, not going beyond the boundaries of a unit severely constraints the grounded theory and its completeness.

As an example of such unit busting we have Glaser's and Strauss' shift from conceptual treatment of one type of ward to a conceptual treatment of another type of ward. One such shift – in the framework of the same hospital – was already

---

12 For the implications of this change for theory testing see (Walker – Cohen 1985).

mentioned above; yet another shift had an even larger geo-graphical scope (1967, 24–25):

> [D]ying of cancer in America can be characterized as oc-curring in a "closed awareness context" ... In a Japanese hospital we once visited, cancer patients typically know they are dying (an "open awareness context"). Why? Because the hospital ward is openly labeled "Cancer." The patient entering the ward reads a clear clue that makes him aware that he is dying. While in America the cues tend to be vague and fleeting, we discovered through the Japanese example that they can be clear even at the beginning stage of a long term of dying. Until then, we had not realized that cues can vary in clarity at the beginning of such a disease as cancer ... This comparative data from Japan stimulated us to find locations in America where clear cues are provided at the start of dying. We found that in a veterans' hospital and in a prison medical ward, patients from the outset were given clear cues that they had cancer.

4.2 Grounded theory on induction, deduction and abduction

In (Strübing 2007, 595) the following figure was given to ex-press the cyclical movement between theory construction and data collection based on theoretical sampling. This cyclical movement should involve three types of inference: induction, deduction and abduction.

Fig. 4: J. Strübing on the unity of inductive, deductive and abductive inferences in the logic of research performed in the grounded type of theory

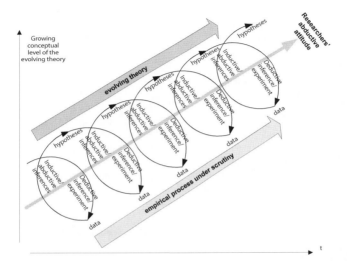

The types of inference being involved in the tradition of grounded theory are quite often mentioned. Already in *Awareness of Dying* Glaser and Strauss declared the following: "Clearly, a substantive theory that is faithful to the everyday realities of the substantive area is one that is carefully induced from diverse data gathered over a considerable period" (1965b, 261). And, at the same time, they voice the following strong objections against employing deduction in order to derive a substantive theory from a formal theory (1965b, 261):[13]

_____

13 For similar objections see (Charmaz 1983, 110).

The use of logical deduction rests on the assumption that the formal theory supplies all the necessary concepts and hypotheses; the consequences are a typical forcing and distorting of data to fit categories of the deduced substantive theory, and the neglecting of relevant data which seem not to fit or cannot be forced into the preexisting sociological categories.

Glaser's and Strauss' emphasis on the method of induction as the primary form of inference given in the grounded type of theory is voiced also in *Discovery of Grounded Theory*. Here they declare that "one canon of judging the usefulness of theory is how it was generated—and we suggest that it is likely to be a better theory to the degree that it has been inductively developed from social research" (1967, 5).

Induction, they claim, should be involved in the method of constant comparison. The latter (1967, 113–114)

makes probable the achievement of a complex theory that corresponds closely to the data, since constant comparisons force the analyst to consider much diversity in data. By *diversity* we mean that each incident is compared with another incident, or with properties of a category, in terms of as many similarities and differences as possible ... This is an inductive method of theory development. To make theoretical sense of so much diversity in his data, the analyst is forced to develop ideas on a level of generality higher in conceptual abstraction than the qualitative material being analyzed.

Glaser in (1978) differentiates between inductive logic and deductive logic, where both are at work in sociological research and where "grounded theory is, of course, inductive; a theory is induced or emerged after data collection starts" (1978, 37).[14]

At the same time he views deduction as being involved in the construction of a grounded type of theory (1978, 38):

---

14 For similar views see also (Glaser 1992, 15–16).

> *Deductive work in grounded theory is used to derive from induced codes conceptual guides* as to where to go next for which comparative group or subgroup, in order to sample for more data to generate theory ... deduction is in the service of further induction and the *source* of derivation are the codes derived from comparing data, *not* deductions from pre-existing theories in the extant literature. To repeat, the focus of deduction is on more comparisons for discovery, not on deriving an hypothesis for verification.

His general characterization of the simultaneous employment of induction and deduction is then as follows (1978, 41):

> To summarily discard deductive elaborating as a tool for discovery is clearly unwise. It is vital in the constant comparative analysis of data for generating theory. To write about the subtle interplay of deductive and inductive generating is not easy. The analyst need only remember that the deductive is in service of an inductive method; it is subservient to it, and ideas arrived at deductively must be discarded unless grounded ... It is only the doctrinaire researcher who may not allow the inductive to correct deductions and emerge as primary, and who will explain "poor fit" with yet another pre-existing theory.

Strauss, contrary to Glaser, puts deduction into opposition to induction in a much stronger way: "Induction refers to the actions that lead to discovery of an hypothesis ... Deduction consists of drawing implications from hypotheses ... for the purposes of verification" (1987, 11–12).[15]

In addition to viewing induction and deduction (the latter at least partially) as being involved in the grounded type of theory, the more recent literature on this type of theory very often mentions also the method of *abduction*.

---

15 For a similar view see also (Strauss – Corbin 1990, 111).

While Strauss mentions it in a footnote stating: "See the writings of Charles Peirce … whose concept of *abduction* strongly emphasized the crucial role of experience in … first phase of research" (1987, 12), Charmaz employs the term "abduction" as follows (Charmaz 2006, 103–104):

> The particular form of reasoning invoked in grounded theory makes it an abductive method, because grounded theory includes *reasoning* about experience for making theoretical conjectures and then checking them through further experience. Abductive reasoning about the data starts with the data and subsequently moves toward hypothesis formation. In brief, abductive inference entails considering all possible theoretical explanations for the data, forming hypotheses for each possible explanation, checking them empirically by examining data, and pursuing the most plausible explanation.

And in a note she adds that abductive reasoning "underlies the pragmatist tradition of problem solving" (Charmaz 2006, 122). At the same time she relates the employment of deduction to the following characteristics of the sociology which was dominant in the US in the 1950s and 1960s (2006, 4–5):

> Beliefs in a unitary method of systematic observation, replicable experiments, operational definitions of concepts, logically deduced hypotheses, and confirmed evidence—often taken as *the* scientific method—formed the assumptions upholding quantitative methods. These assumptions supported positivism, the dominant paradigm of inquiry in routine natural science. Mid-century positivist conceptions of scientific method and knowledge stressed objectivity, generality, replication of research, and falsification of competing hypotheses and theories. Social researchers['] … beliefs in scientific logic, a unitary method, objectivity, and truth legitimized reducing qualities of human experience to quantifiable variables … As positivism gained strength in mid-century, the division between theory and research simultaneously grew. Growing numbers of

quantitative researchers concentrated on obtaining concrete information. Those quantitative researchers who connected theory and research tested logically deduced hypotheses from an existing theory. Although they refined extant theory, their research seldom led to new theory construction.

There are at least three deficiencies in these claims trying to link induction and abduction to the grounded type of theory, while relating deduction to positivism and quantification.

First, deduction is viewed as somehow internally (necessarily and inseparably) related to positivist philosophy, to views on methods of natural and social sciences inspired by this philosophy and to a quantitatively oriented sociology. The truth, however is, that logical deduction is the subjected matter of modern logic which, to state it succinctly, is nothing more, nor less than a *science dealing with the issue of entailment* and is in no way inherently related to positivism or to any type of methodology.

Second, in those claims, a precise characterization of induction, deduction and abduction as three types of inferences is either completely absent or holding to a terminology, viewed as outdated from the point of view of modern logic and methodology, of the particular (lower level of generality as compared to) and general (higher level of generality). So for example, Glaser's and Strauss' claim stated above that by means of induction one can "develop ideas on a level of generality higher in conceptual abstraction than the qualitative material being analyzed" (1967, 114) echoes the claim that *in an inductive inference the premises are of a lower level of generality compared to that of the conclusion.*

Charmaz also holds to this outdated attempt to classify types reasoning by employing the terminology of lower and higher level of generality. She characterizes deduction as "a type of reasoning that starts with the general and abstract concept and reasons to the specific instances" (2006, 187).

Third, claims on induction, deduction and abduction appearing in literature on grounded theory never show how they are actually employed in actual sociological practice. Instead one encounters here, on the one hand, just a general talk about these types of inferences and, on the other hand, concrete cases of sociological research in the tradition of grounded theory.

Let me now try to remedy these weaknesses.

5. Induction, Deduction and Abduction

In this part I clarify the nature of deduction, induction and abduction by drawing on the more recent logical and methodological literature.

5.1 Grounded theory's ambitions, argument, reasoning, entailment, etc.

The overall ambition of the tradition of the grounded type of sociological theory is "the discovery of theory from data systematically obtained from social research" (Glaser – Strauss 1967, 2), and where under "discovery of theory" one understands in this tradition that "one generates conceptual categories or their properties from evidence" (Glaser – Strauss 1967, 23).

This discovery should, once viewed as a gradual introduction of categories and of properties of categories, stand for a process of a sequential construction of theory so that the latter would gradually become more and more conceptually dense.

This means, on the one hand, that one lacks, before interacting with an area under investigation, a theory pertaining to this area and, on the other hand, the collection of data in the course of this interaction serves the purpose of constructing a theory for this area. The construction of such a theory can then be viewed as an accomplishment of a kind of *logic of discovery* in the sense of "logical reasoning whose premises are a set of empirical phenomena and whose conclusion is an explanatory hypothesis" (Kelle 1990, 39).

In addition to the term "reasoning" appearing in the last quote, another term relevant for the relation of conclusion to premises is that of "argument."[16] Under the latter logic understands an act where from a finite number of propositions one derives a proposition, and where the former are labeled as "premises" and the latter as "conclusion."[17] Stated otherwise, an argument stands for a pair composed of set of propositions labeled "premises" and a proposition labeled "conclusion."

What in an argument can also appear are the so-called propositional forms in the sense of a linguistic scheme with variables which once valuated yield propositions. Propositions and propositional forms together make up the class of propositional expressions. On the basis of the latter one can then introduces the term *entailment* in the sense of a relation between a set M of propositional expressions and a propositional expression W, and where this relation fulfills certain conditions depending on the types of entailment being at work.

The difference between reasoning and argument can be tentatively delineated by means of the following comparison:[18]

Reasoning stands for a process of arriving at conclusions from evidence, enabling the formation of, for example, hypotheses, solving a practical problem standing for a case of "constructive thinking." This evidence, in the context of a given knowledge, should by reasoning, yield those hypotheses, solve that problem, etc.	*Argument* stands for inference from a set of propositional expressions as premises to a propositional expression as conclusion, so that this inference fulfills certain conditions in order for it to be an entailment in the sense that the premises entail the conclusion.

---

16 Here I have utilized (Cmorej 2000). For a more detailed analysis of reasoning based on the analysis of an actor's stock of knowledge undergoing in this reasoning some changes see (Levi 1996).

17 Under "proposition" I understand "meaning of declarative sentence."

18 Here I found (Fritz 1960, 126–127) to be very useful.

From this comparison it is obvious that reasoning in addition to arguments involves also some additional elements like observation reports and, as I will show below, definitions. The logical validity of reasoning cannot thus be ascertained in direct manner, but several additional mediating steps are necessary before its structure can be understood as a chain of arguments. To the latter I therefore assign here priority in the sequence of my explications.

Finally, because in the tradition of the grounded type of theory the type of reasoning involved should yield a set of concepts (categories and properties of categories) which is gradually extended in each step of reasoning, two additional terms related to reasoning are worth introducing here: ampliativity and monotonicity.

Ampliativity characterizes reasoning in which the conclusion goes beyond the content (knowledge) given in the premises. *Monotonicity* characterizes reasoning in which the enlargement of premises of reasoning by additional information does not invalidate its conclusion derived before this enlargement. A standard example for the violation of monotonocity in Artificial Intelligence circles is the following one (Brewka 1991). If we know that the individual labeled "Tweety" is a bird, we infer the conclusion that Tweety can fly, since birds typically fly. But by introducing into the premises of our reasoning the additional information that Tweety is a penguin, we invalidate our former conclusion.

Let me now confront that ambition of the tradition of grounded type of theory and the possible existence of logic of discovery with the characteristics of induction, deduction, and abduction as they are delineated in the more recent literature on logic and methodology.

5.2 Deduction

Modern logic understands deduction as a type of argument in which there exists between the set M of propositional expressions given in the premises and the propositional expression W given in the conclusion the relation of *logical entailment*. This relation between M and W is given if and only if a situation cannot obtain when all elements of M were true (or become true under substitution turning them into propositions) and W were not true (would not become true under this substitution). Expressed elliptically, truth is "preserved" or "transferred" in the course of deduction of W from M.

For a deductive argument holds that if one adds into its premises an additional propositional expression without deleting any other, the validity of the argument is not violated. So, *deductive arguments are by their very nature monotonic*.

Additional light is shed on deduction when it is characterized as a way of *reasoning*. Here I mean that the information/knowledge given in the conclusion of a deduction does not go beyond the information/knowledge given in the premises, that is, *deductive reasoning is nonampliative* or, stated otherwise, *epistemically sterile*.

For a better understanding of the nature of deduction with respect to reasoning as given in framework of the grounded type of theory, let me mention Peirce's delineation of deduction. In his early period he gives the following well known example of deduction (CP 2.623):[19]

---

19 I use here the standard system of reference to Peirce *Collected Papers*, CP for short. The first digit gives the volume and the next three give the number of paragraph in the respective volume.

All the beans from this bag are white
These beans are from this bag
These beans are white

Using syllogistic notation, the structure of deduction can be expressed as follows (5.276):

If A, then B;
But A:
$\therefore B$.

In the notation of predicate calculus that structure can be expressed as follows:[20]

$\forall x\ (Ax \rightarrow Bx)$
Aa
Ba

Both transcriptions employing logical notations bring to the fore a feature of deduction which is crucial with respect to reasoning given in the grounded type of theory. Here I mean that in both transcriptions one substitutes for symbol "B" in the premise the same name as for symbol "B" in the conclusion, and where *this name has in the premise and in the conclusion one and the same meaning*. So, deduction is not only epistemically but also *semantically sterile*. This meaning-conservativism of deduction clearly contradicts the above reconstructed cyclical nature of construction of a grounded type of theory. As shown above, the understanding of certain characteristics of the area under investigation is subjected to a reinterpretation once they are understood in that construction as properties of certain categories.

---

20 "$\forall x$" stands for "for all x"; "$\rightarrow$" stands for the sentential connective "if ____, then ____".

5.3 Induction

Induction as a method of inquiry is assigned an important role in the tradition of grounded type of theory, at least at the level of declarations of its proponents. For example, according to Strauss, induction as a method of inquiry "refers to the actions that lead to discovery of a hypothesis – that is having a hunch or an idea, then converting it into a hypothesis and assessing whether it might provisionally work as at least partial condition for a type of event, act, relationship, strategy, etc." (1987, 11–12).

Induction displays the following three characteristics.[21] First, in an inductive argument its premises entail its conclusion not with logical necessity but (only) with a certain degree of probability or, stated otherwise, the premises make their conclusion probable (Salmon 1966, 8). Thus, it holds that even if the premises are true (turn into true propositions under a certain substitution), the conclusion could still be false (could turn into a false proposition under this substitution). Second, an inductive type of argument is nonmonotonic; the introduction of additional propositions into the premises can invalidate the truth of a conclusion derived before from the as yet nonenlarged set of premises. Third, inductive reasoning is ampliative in the sense that the information/knowledge given in its conclusion goes above and beyond the information/knowledge given in its premises.

This threefold characterization of induction can be further specified by dealing with different types of inductive reasoning. One type stands for reasoning from particular cases, via *enumeration*, to a hypothesis, as it is in the famous white-swan example. Another type stands for reasoning aiming at the creation of a hypothesis, but not by enumeration, but

---

21 Here I have benefited from (Viceník 2001) and (Fritz 1960).

by *elimination* of other hypotheses.[22] While the purpose of employing any of these types is *discovery* of a hypothesis, methodology identifies yet another purpose of employment of inductive reasoning, namely, *confirmation* of an already given hypothesis.

By viewing both enumeration and elimination as *applied methods* and by viewing the orientation towards hypothesis-discovery and hypothesis-confirmation as *purposes* of employing inductive arguments, one obtains the following table listing some of the representatives of the respective view on inductive reasoning:[23]

Table 5: Typology for inductive reasoning

Purpose of induct. argument / Method applied in inductive argument	Discovery of hypothesis	Confirmation of hypothesis
enumeration	Aristotle	Carnap, Reichenbach
elimination	Francis Bacon, J. S. Mill	Keynes

Because my analysis focuses on the methodology of the grounded type of theory whose orientation is clearly on discovery of hypothesis, I need not deal here with the approaches to inductive reasoning listed in the right column.

---

22 For a differentiation between these two types of induction see (Barker 1957, 48–90).

23 Here I benefited from (Riemer 1988) and (Barker 1957). On Aristotle see his *First Analytics* (Book II, Chapter 23); on J. S. Mill see his (1974); on Carnap see his (1950; 1952), on Reichenbach see his (1949) and on Keynes see his (1921).

Nor is it necessary for me to deal with inductive reasoning aiming at the discovery of a hypothesis by means of enumeration. There are at least four reasons for this.

Enumeration is here understood as a listing of instantiations of certain characteristics, say, of properties like being white and being a swan. This method is thus completely opposed to the practice of the grounded type of theory. First, because in this practice one does not look for a repeated appearance of certain characteristics, but tries to generate categories from certain characteristics as found in an initially pregiven set of data. Second, in this practice it does not make any sense to look continually for the same data to generate continually the same categories. Instead, one tries to generate from a pregiven set of data as many as possible disparate categories and different properties of these categories. Third, the very idea of looking for the same characteristics presuppose that we *know* them, that is, we have in vocabulary a set of expressions with a pregiven meaning, otherwise we could not look for their reappearance.

Fourth, in the course of the derivation of the conclusion from the premises no new names referring to new characteristics are introduced. This is readily seen when one looks at Peirce's bag-and-bean example for induction (CP 2.623):

These beans are from this bag
These beans are white
All the beans from this bag are white

In both premises and conclusions we refer to the same entities: bag, beans and white color, while in the conclusion, with respect to the premises from which it was derived, no new names for new entities appear. That is, discovery-induction based on the method of enumeration is, like deduction, *semantically sterile*.

Is discovery-induction based on the method of enumeration, like deduction, also *epistemically* sterile? A quick glance at Peirce's bag-and-bean example indicates that in the course of induction by means of enumeration, knowledge about what state of affairs is given in certain location changes into a knowledge-claim, even if, with a hypothetical status, about what the state is in another location. So, discovery-induction based on the method of enumeration is not, contrary to deduction, epistemically sterile. However, measured by the ambitions of the grounded type of theory – to discover new categories and their properties – discovery-induction based on the method of enumeration is *epistemically shallow*.[24]

Let me now turn to Francis Bacon's non-enumerative approach to inductive reasoning.[25] He views his endeavor as belonging to logic, declaring "in this Organon of ours we are dealing with logic … But our logic instructs the understanding and trains it … to dissect nature truly, and to discover the powers and actions of bodies and their laws limned in matter" (Aph. LII). This logic he views as opposed to logic prevailing in his time; "logic in its present state is useless for the discovery of sciences … current logic is good for establishing and fixing errors … rather than inquiring into truth; hence it is not useful" (Aph. XI & XII).

The logic he proposes draws fundamentally on the conceptual pair *form* and *nature*. The reason for which he chooses

---

24 This was expressed by Psillos as follows: "Enumerative induction … operates with the principle 'garbage in, garbage out': the descriptive vocabulary of the conclusion cannot be different from that of the premises" (2011, 122).

25 Here I found very useful (Ajdukiewicz 1955), (Filkorn 1974) and (Horton 1973). All quotes are from Book II of (Bacon 2003); the Roman numeral gives the number of the aphorism, "Aph." for short.

this pair is as follows: "The task and purpose of human Power is to generate and superinduce on a given body a new nature or new natures. The task and purpose of human Science is to find for a given nature its Form, or true difference, or causative nature or the source of its coming-to-be" (Aph. I). With regard to the concept of form he declares (Aph. XVII)

> When we speak of forms, we mean simply those laws and limitations of pure act which organise and constitute a simple nature, like heat, light or weight, in every kind of susceptible material and subject. The form of heat therefore or the form of light is the same thing as the law of heat or the law of light.

In a next step he characterizes the relation of form and nature of a thing in the following three fold way. First, "the form of a nature is such that if it is there, the given nature inevitably follows. Hence it is always present when the nature is present; it universally affirms it, and is in the whole of it" (Aph. 4).

Second, "The same form is such that when it is taken away, the given nature inevitably disappears. And therefore it is always absent when that nature is absent, and its absence always implies the absence of that nature, and it exists only in that nature" (Aph. IV).

Third, (Aph. XIII):

> We must make a presentation to the intellect of instances in which the nature under investigation exists to a certain degree. This may be done by comparing the increase and decrease in the same subject, or by comparing different subjects with another ... a nature is not accepted as a true form unless it always decreases when the nature itself decreases, and likewise always increases when the nature itself increases.

Based on this threefold characterization he proposes the following three-step procedure enabling him to state in the form of axioms the relations between the nature and form of things (Aph. X):

[1.] We must compile a good, adequate natural and experimental history. This is the foundation of the matter. We must not invent or imagine what nature does or suffers; we must discover it.

[2.] A natural and experimental history is so diverse and disconnected that it confounds and confuses the understanding unless it is stopped short, and presented in an appropriate order. So tables must be drawn up and a coordination of instances made, in such a way and with such organisation that the mind may be able to act upon them.

[3.] Even with these, the mind, left to itself and moving of its own accord, is incompetent and unequal to the formation of axioms unless it is governed and directed. And therefore, in the third place, a true and proper induction must be supplied.

It seems appropriate at this point to analyze the methods pertaining to the second step. He characterizes these methods as follows (Aph. XI & XII & XIII; italics are mine – I. H.):

[F]irst for any given nature one must make a presentation to the intellect of all known instances which meet in the same nature, however disparate the materials may be ... We call this the *table of existence and presence* ...

Secondly, we must make a presentation to the intellect of instances which are devoid of a given nature; because (as has been said) the form ought no less to be absent when a given nature is absent than present when it is present. But this would be infinite if we took them all. And therefore we should attach negatives to our affirmatives, and investigate absences only in subjects which are closely related to others in which a given nature exists and appears. This we have chosen to call the *table of divergence, or of closely related absences* ...

Thirdly, we must make a presentation to the intellect of instances in which the nature under investigation exists to a certain degree. This may be done by comparing the increase and decrease in the same subject, or by comparing different subjects with another. A nature is not accepted as a true form unless it always decreases when the nature itself decreases, and likewise always increases when the nature itself increases. We have chosen to call such a table a *table of degrees or table of comparison*.

For a better understanding of the nature of these three tables, I represent them schematically as follows (a_1, a_2 and a_3 stand for three instances of objects under investigation; A, B, C, D, E, F, G stand for different forms; N stands for a nature):[26]

Fig. 5: Bacon's table of existence/presence

$$a_1, A, B, C, D, E, N$$
$$a_2, A, B, C, D, F, N$$
$$a_3, A, B, C, D, G, N$$

Based on this table we have to eliminate forms E, F, and G so they do not exist in all cases where N exists; we are thus left with forms A, B, C, D. Next we apply to them the method of divergence/absence ("¬" symbolizes the absence of a form and of nature, respectively).

Fig. 6: Bacon's table of divergence/closely related absences

$$a_1, \neg A, \neg B, C, \neg D \ \neg N$$
$$a_2, \neg A, \neg B, C, D, \neg N$$
$$a_3, \neg A, \neg B, C, \neg D, \neg N$$

---

26 I have utilized here figures from (Ajdukiewicz 1955, XVI–LII) and from (Filkorn 1974).

We have to eliminate form C because it is present in all cases where N is absent; we are then left with forms A, B, and D. Next we subject these three forms to the test of degrees; here we set up one table for cases when N increases and another when N decreases ("+" and "−" as subscripts indicate an increase and decrease, respectively).

Fig. 7a: Bacon's table of degrees – N increases

$$a_1, A_+, B_-, D_+, N_+$$
$$a_2, A_+, B_-, D_+, N_+$$
$$a_3, A_+, B, D_+, N_+$$

Fig. 7b: Bacon's table of degrees/comparison – N decreases

$$a_1, A_-, D_+, N_-$$
$$a_2, A_-, D, N_-$$
$$a_3, , A_-, D, N_-$$

Based on Table 7a we have to eliminate form B because it either decreases or does not change in all cases where N always increases. Finally, based on Table 7b we have to eliminate also form D so as it increases or does not change in all cases in which N decreases. We are thus left with form A as the basic form for the nature N.

Let me now compare Bacon's approach with the methods viewed as central in the grounded type of theory.

Seemingly, one could object to the requirement that "one must make a presentation to the intellect of all known instances which meet in the same nature" (Aph. XI), because from the very beginning of research, the number of instances known to exist is usually very high. The methods of the grounded type of theory bypass this problem by delimiting the instances of a subject matter of research to just few or even one. So, for example, to one ward, namely, the cancer ward in one hospital, were it investigates into one subject-matter, namely, awareness of dying. And the research remains in this framework until the first categories and properties of categories emerge. Only then the researcher can shift, say, to another ward (e.g., emergency ward) or even to other hospitals, investigating there into the awareness of dying.

There are, however, at least two features of Bacon's approach to induction which diverge completely from the methods in the grounded type of theory. First, as indicated by the four Baconian tables, we have to have in advance, before compiling them, already at our disposal the terms A through H for the forms as well term N for the nature. So, from this point of view, the situation is similar to that in enumerative induction: eliminative induction in its Baconian understanding is, like enumerative induction, *semantically sterile*.

Second (having of course in mind that grounded theory's orientation is to quality) in order to be able to relate in the third and fourth Baconian tables the degrees of forms A, B and D to the degrees of nature N, *we have to have in advance knowledge enabling us to find out that these forms and this nature at all vary*.

Thus, if we try via experiments to find out, for example, if variation of temperature of a pregiven set of bodies made from the same substance is related to variation of their length, *before* performing such experiments we need to have at our disposal, in addition to the terms *temperature* and *length*, methods for finding out if a variation of temperature has taken place and a variation of length have taken place.[27]

---

27 This holds for Bacon's experiments trying to find for a substance the ratio of volume of its solid state to that of its gaseous state (Aph. XL, Book II).

Eliminative induction in its Baconian understanding, contrary to enumerative induction, is however *not epistemically shallow*. The reason for this lies in the fact that it enables, based on the prior knowledge of methods enabling to find out that the form A and the nature N have varied, to relate these variations. And once these variations are quantified by means of two scales, one for the change of A and one for the change of N, *one obtains a new method for quantifying N by means of A and vice versa.*

Let me now turn to Peirce's understanding of induction.[28] This understanding and his understanding of reasoning in general can be differentiated into an earlier period, spanning the period from the mid 1860s approximately to the end of the century and a later period spanning the first decade of the 20th century.

My argument focuses on the changes in his understanding of induction and of hypothesis, later labeled as "abduction." The latter will be dealt with below. Schematically these changes and the relations between the former and latter understanding of the respective types of inferences can be expressed schematically as follows (Riemer 1988, 48):

Fig. 8: Changes in Peirce's understanding of types of inferences and their relations

28 Here I have benefited from (Cheng 1969) and (Reimer 1988). I abstract from the fact that Peirce characterizes induction as well as deduction, hypothesis and abduction interchangeable as "argument," "reasoning" and "inference."

In Peirce's *early period*, the starting point of his understanding of induction is the delineation of the nature of inference by the following characterization of its structure: "Every inference involves the judgment that, if such propositions as the premises are true, then a proposition related to them, as the conclusion is, must be, or is likely to be true" (CP 2.462).

He identifies, in addition to the premises and conclusion, in the structure of an argument also the so-called "leading principle" (*L*, for short) in the sense of a rule which relates premises and conclusion. This structure thus is (CP 2.466)

L and P
$\therefore C$

By means of L he can also classify arguments, namely, that once L and P are true, then they make the truth of C either necessary, as in the case of deduction, or probable, as in the case of induction (CP 2.466). This classification can be expressed schematically as follows (CP 2.623):

Fig. 9: Peirce's 1878 classification of inferences

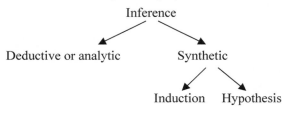

At the basis of such a classification is the idea that deduction is explicative (analytic) in the sense that (CP 2.680)

> certain facts are first laid down in the premises ... Now, the facts being ... laid down, some order among some of them, not particularly made use of for the purpose of stating them,

may perhaps be discovered; and this will enable us to throw part or all of them into a new statement, the possibility of which might have escaped attention. Such a statement will be the conclusion of an analytic inference.

Contrary to the explicative inferences which yield new results primarily in a *psychological* sense (say, because they escaped the attention of the persons actually performing the inferences), there exists a category of synthetic reasoning where "the facts summed up in the conclusion are not among those stated in the premises. They are different facts ... These are the only inferences which increase our real knowledge" (CP 2.680). Inferences belonging to this category are thus by their very nature *ampliative* (2.636).

In addition to the bag-and-bean example for induction given above he states also the following formula for induction (CP 2.511):

S', S'', S''', etc. are taken as random as *M*'s;
S', S'', S''', etc. are *P*.
Any *M* is probably *P*.

From that example, as well as from this formula, it is obvious that early Peirce viewed the conclusion of induction as a scientific law; this corresponds to his claim that one of the aims of science is "the discovery of Laws, which is accomplished by induction" (CP 2.713).

Against Peirce's approach to induction as delineated above I could state, with respect to the methods given in the grounded type of theory, the same charges as were offered against Bacon's approach to enumerative induction and also valuate it in the same manner, namely, as being *semantically sterile* but *not epistemically shallow*. These charges and evaluation could, however, be viewed as being performed with respect to the grounded type of theory, that is, from the "outside," so to say, and thus as irrelevant for that approach.

In order to show that this is not so and that Peirce's approach to induction in his early years inherently contains important limitations, I turn now to one aspect of his approach, namely, "predesignation," which should have the status of a requirement to be fulfilled by any valid inductive inference.

With respect to the above given formula for induction the term "predesignation" is understood as follows: "If in sampling any class, say the M's, we first decide what the character P is for which we propose to sample this class" (CP 2.737). And, in general, it should hold: "The induction has its full force when the character concerned has been designated before examining the sample" (CP 6.413). That is, before making an inference corresponding by its structure to the structure schematically represented by that formula, we have to know in advance what are the *references* of expressions we substitute for "P," otherwise we could not pick up the respective sample. And in order to know these references we have to know in advance the *meanings* of these expressions.

The reason why Peirce imposes on valid inductive inferences the requirement of predesignation was spelled out by C.-Y. Cheng as follows (1969, 48):

> Peirce's argument for the necessity of predesignation for the validity of induction is as follows. Suppose we were to draw our inference without predesignation of the character P ....then according to Peirce, we might always find a character which belongs merely to a group of instances examined, and does not belong to the whole population from which the group of instances examined is taken. It is always theoretically possible to find a common character or characters in any given group of things belonging only to that group of things. Without predesignation, our post-designate character may be just

such a common character and very often it is. If it is, it would be an inadequate basis for making an inductive conclusion.

In support of his requirement of predesignation Peirce gives the following example (CP 2.738). He takes a biographical dictionary and picks out the name of the first five poets whose name starts with the letter "A" together with information about the age at which they died. To the numbers stating their age he applies a sequence of mathematical operations and finds out that they yield for each of those five poets the same triple of numbers. It is, however, sure that "there is not the smallest reason to believe that the next poet's age would possess the same characters" (CP 2.738)

Despite the persuasiveness of this example, what still is hidden behind Peirce's predesignation is a view on the aim of scientific cognition which I label as a *drive of methodologist dealing with induction towards the universality of statements found by inductive reasoning and where this universality is understood by them as uniformity*.

By the term uniformity I understand here that a characteristic discovered as common to entities sampled from a group should hold also for entities from another group from which as yet no samples were drawn. For a better understanding of that drive, let me compare it with the approach of the grounded type of theory to sampling as delineated in (Glaser – Strauss 1967) and (Glaser 1978).

In the former one encounters the following claim (1967, 23):

A concept may be generated from one fact, which then becomes merely one of a universe of many possible indicators for, or data on, the concept ... In discovering theory, one generates conceptual categories, or their properties from evidence; then the evidence from which the category emerged is used to illustrate the concept. The evidence may not necessarily be accurate beyond a doubt ... but the concept is undoubtedly a relevant abstraction about what is going on in the area studied. Furthermore, the concept itself will not change, while even the most accurate facts can change. Concepts only have their meanings respecified at time because their theoretical and research purposes have evolved.

The important methodological consequences of such a search for both similarities and differences are then spelled out as follows (1967, 37–38):

While the verification of theory aims at establishing a relatively few major uniformities and variations on the same conceptual level, we believe that the generation of theory should aim at achieving much *diversity* in emergent categories ... This position on the diversity of conceptual level has important consequences for the sociologist and sociology. As the sociologist uses standard sociological concepts, he soon discovers that they usually become very differently defined, dimensioned, specified, or typed. Typical boundaries of the standard concept become broken. Furthermore, the boundaries of the established battery of sociological concepts are also broken.

This means that sampling, once driven by the already emerged categories and properties of categories does not stand only for a search for data to which they can be uniformly applied, but also for data to which they cannot be uniformly applied which then, in turn, enables to derive new properties of categories as well as to introduce new categories.

This feature of the grounded type of theory is viewed by Glaser and Strauss as being opposed to theorizing standardly used in sociology in the 1960s. This theorizing (1967, 63)

claims generality of scope; that is, one assumes that if the relationship holds for one group under certain conditions, it will probably hold for other groups under the same conditions. This assumption of persistence is subjected only to being disproven—not proven—when other sociologists question its credibility … Persistence helps to generate scope but it is usually considered uninteresting, since it requires no modification of the theory.

The search for diversity, when comparing different groups, (Glaser 1978, 42)

has the purpose of generating theory … if important differences … also exist between the groups, they become part of the analysis as qualifying conditions of the general hypothesis or idea that emerged from the initial comparison. These differences do not disqualify a comparison, they enrich it. Comparing the apparently non-comparable increases the broad range of groups and ideas available to the emerging theory.

This purpose is symptomatic of what Glaser and Strauss label as *logic of ongoing inclusion of groups* and where this logic should be a feature by which the grounded type of theory differs from the sociological theorizing standardly used in the 1960s. The latter's logic should be (1967, 50–51)

one of preplanned inclusion and exclusion, [it] warns the analyst from comparing "non-comparable" groups. To be included in the planned set, a group must have "enough features in common" with the other groups. To be excluded, it must show a "fundamental difference" from the others. These two rules represent an attempt to "hold constant" strategic facts, or to disqualify groups where the facts either cannot actually be held constant or would introduce more unwanted differences … To be sure, these rules of comparability are important when accurate evidence is the goal but they hinder the generation of theory, in which "non-comparability" of groups is irrelevant. They prevent the use of a much wider range of groups for developing properties of categories.

All these reflections yield in the framework of the grounded type of theory the following differentiation between two types of sampling, namely, *theoretical sampling* symptomatic for that type of theory and *statistical sampling* viewed by Glaser and Strauss as used in the standard sociological theorizing (1967, 62–63):

Theoretical sampling is done in order to discover categories and their properties, and to suggest the interrelationships into a theory ... The adequate theoretical sample is judged on the basis of how widely and diversely the analyst chose his groups for saturating categories according to the type of theory he wished to develop ... The inadequate theoretical sample is easily spotted, since the theory associated with it is usually thin and not well integrated, and has too many obvious unexplained exceptions.

Statistical sampling is done to obtain accurate evidence on distributions of people among categories to be used in descriptions or verifications ... The adequate statistical sample ... is judged on the basis of techniques of random and stratified sampling used in relation to social structure of a group or groups sampled. The inadequate statistical sample ... must be pointed out by specialists in methodology, since other researchers tend to accept technical sophistication uncritically.

It is exactly the statistical type of sampling which became the subject matter of investigation in Peirce's *late approach* to induction, namely, *quantitative* induction which he views as a method of testing statistical hypotheses; it "investigates the interrogative suggestion of retroduction, "What is the 'real probability' that an individual member of a certain experimental class, say the S's, will have a certain character, say that of being P?"" (CP 2.758). Here retroduction stands for abduction; I will deal with it below.

In addition to quantitative type, Peirce speaks about *crude* induction and *qualitative* induction.[29] Any of these three

---

29 On these see (Riemer 1988).

types stands for an inference from characteristics of a sample to characteristics of all elements of this group. In the light of the aims of my study, the following three late-Peircean characteristics which hold for any of these three types of induction are worth quoting:

> [1.] The induction adds nothing. At the very most it corrects the value of a ratio or slightly modifies a hypothesis in a way which has already been contemplated as possible (CP 7.217).
> [2.] The only thing that induction accomplishes is to determine the value of a quantity. It sets out with a theory and it measures the degree of concordance of that theory with fact. It never can originate any idea whatever (CP 5.145).
> [3.] [T]he only sound procedure for induction, whose business consists in testing a hypothesis already recommended by the retroductive procedure, is to receive its suggestions from the hypothesis first, to take up the predictions of experience which it conditionally makes, and then try the experiment and see whether it turns out as it was virtually predicted in the hypothesis that it would (CP 2.755).

Thus, late-Peircean understanding of induction does not correspond to the type of reasoning given in the grounded type of theory. The latter's focus being primarily on theory generation; the former's, on the contrary, on testing of a given theory with its pregiven vocabulary with pregiven meanings.

From this follows the conclusion *that all types of induction dealt with above are semantically sterile*. This corresponds to the view presented in (Hindricks – Fay 1999), namely, that the vocabulary of hypothesis conjectured by induction "always lies within the … vocabulary specified by the evidence language" (1999, 272). However, as quoted already above, one of the important features of the grounded type of theory is that the movement from data to categories and properties of categories stands for a "meaning making activity" (Glaser 1998, 140). Thus, we are still in need of methodological reconstruction of a type of reasoning which is not semantically conservative. Hindricks and Fay view abduction as such a type of reasoning because the latter "in some sense outputs hypotheses transcending the vocabulary of the evidence language" (1999, 272). Let me find out if this really holds.

5.4 Abduction

In the works of Peirce one can find several claims pertaining not only to deduction and induction, but also to a third type of reasoning which he labeled initially as "hypothesis" and later as "abduction."[30] I list four of them.

> [1.] All the ideas of science come to it by way of abduction. Abduction consists of studying facts and devising a theory to explain them. (CP 5.145)
> [2.] Abduction is the process of forming explanatory hypotheses. It is the only logical operation which introduces any new ideas. (CP 5.172)
> [3.] It must be remembered that abduction ... is logical inference ... having a definite logical form. (CP 5.188)
> [4.] The surprising fact, C, is observed. But if A were true, C would be a matter of course. Hence, there is reason to suspect that A is true. (CP 5.189)

And, again, as in the treatment of induction and deduction, Peirce gives the bag-and-bean example for that third type of reasoning (CP 2.623)

---

30 Here I found useful (Riemer 1988). For details on the development of Peirce's approach to hypothesis and abduction see also (Anderson 1986), (Burks 1946) and (Psillos 2011). For the relation of Peirce's views on hypothesis and induction to Aristotle see (Kempski 1992a), (Hilpinen 2000) and (Flores 2014).

All the beans from this bag are white,
These beans are white;
These beans are from this bag.

If we now look at Table 5 above, for all types of induction listed there holds that they stand for a non-deductive type of reasoning. The importance of Peirce's introduction of the terms "hypothesis" and "abduction" is that he did not hold to the converse claim, namely, that all non-deductive types of reasoning are by their nature inductive. This is readily seen in Figure 9 above, where Peirce splits synthetic inferences into induction and hypothesis.

This split can also be detected in his delineation of the form of inference characteristic of hypothesis which is different from that given above for induction. It should be as follows (CP 2.511):

Any M is, for instance, P', P', P'', etc.,
S is P', P', P'', etc.;
S is probably M

In addition, the symbols "P'," "P'," ... as well as "M" are assigned a special epistemic status, namely, the former should stand for characteristics of a phenomenon and the later for their cause. In this sense, reasoning of the hypothesis type is viewed by Peirce as a reasoning from a claim about a phenomenon ("S is P', P', P'', etc.") to a claim about the cause of the characteristics of this phenomenon ("S is probably M.") which has the status of a hypothesis. This corresponds to Peirce's view that one of the tasks of science is "the discovery of cause, which is accomplished by hypothetic inference" (CP 2.713).

This view on the nature of hypothesis as a type of inference is understood by Peirce in his later period in such a way that the derived claim about the cause should represent a *new* proposition but still with the status of a hypothesis. Thus, *abduction should fulfill a discovery-function*.

The form he assigns to abduction should be different from that of hypothesis given above, namely, as follows (Peirce 1975, 182):

If μ were true π, π', π" would follow as miscellaneous consequences –
But true π, π', π" are in fact true;
Provisionally, we may suppose that μ is true.

If we now look at Peirce's approach to what he labels initially as "hypothesis" and later as "abduction," we find out that it contains an inherent contradiction. On the one hand, both should stand, he claims, for a process of discovery and where the result (product) of this discovery should be given in the conclusion of these last two inference-schemes given above. But, on the other hand, the terms appearing in the conclusion of these schemes should already be pregiven in their premises. Thus, in Peirce's understanding of both hypothesis and abduction it is presupposed that *the vocabulary of the conclusion does not go beyond the vocabulary of the premises*.

One arrives at the same result when one turns to both his bag-and-bean example and to the claim listed under number [4.] above. In the former, like in the bag-and-bean examples for deduction and induction given above, the vocabulary of the conclusion does not differ from that of the premises. As to the latter, it is worth noting that Peirce complements that claim as follows: "A cannot be abductively inferred … cannot be abductively conjectured until its entire content is already present in the premise, 'If A were true, C would be a matter of course'" (CP 5.189).

Let me now turn to two more recent papers on abduction, namely, (Aliseda 2003) and (Schurz 2008).

Aliseda models abductive reasoning on the basis of mathematical reasoning, the latter being viewed as a paradigmatic example of classical deductive reasoning characterized by two aspects: certainty, in the sense of the existence of a logically necessary relation between premises and conclusion, and monotonicity in the sense delineated above. Abductive reasoning is then defined as *"deductive reasoning in reverse plus additional conditions"* (2003, 31) where under "reverse" she understands that while in "deductive inference a conclusion follows from a set of premises ... in abduction, the conclusion is the given and premises (or in fact part of them) are the output of an inferential process" (2003, 31).

She also offers another, namely, a methodological characterization of abduction; "Abduction is thinking from evidence to explanation" (2003, 30). As an example of such thinking she gives the example of an attempt to explain the observation of a lawn being wet by considering the fact that it has rained and/or that a sprinkler has been turned on. As the components of a possible explanation-formula α of fact φ she lists the background theory Θ as well as the relevant facts; in that example it is "r" referring to the fact that it rained, "s" that the sprinkler was turned on, while "w" stands for the fact to be explained: that the lawn was wet.

The first requirement she imposes on explanation is the requirement of *inference* symbolically expressed as follows ("$\models$" stands for entailment and "α's" lists possible explanations, "c" stands for children turning a water hose on; "$\&$" stands for conjunction):

Inference: $\Theta, \alpha \models \varphi$
α's: $r, s, c, r \& s, r \& c, r \& c \& s, \Theta \rightarrow w$

It is possible that some explanation has to be ruled out because certain facts did not obtain, say, no children were around in the time when the lawn got wet. Aliseda therefore imposes the requirement of consistency which runs as follows:

Consistence: Θ, α is consistent
α's: r, s, r & s, $\Theta \rightarrow w$

Finally, on the very explanation she imposes two additional requirements: it cannot be performed without a background theory but at the same time it cannot be performed by means of this theory alone:

Explanation: $\Theta \not\models \varphi$, $\alpha \not\models \varphi$
α's: r, s, r & s, $\Theta \rightarrow w$

It is noteworthy that in Aliseda's approach all the components necessary for a possible and then successful explanation are given in advance: the knowledge about the possibly, with respect to the explained fact φ, relevant facts r, s, and c, as well as the background theory Θ. Even if such a situation can be obtained in empirical science, it does not correspond to the practice of the grounded type of theory.

Schurz's paper (2008) presents an interesting typology of abduction which is based on a following two-fold characterization of abduction combined with a differentiation between two functions of abduction. That characterization is as follows: "abductions serve the goal of inferring something about the *unobserved causes* or *explanatory reasons* of the observed events" and "some kinds of abduction *can* introduce new concepts ... I call abductions which introduce new concepts or models *creative*" (2008, 202). As to the two functions of abduction, there is a *justificational* ("inferential") function and a *strategic* ("discovery") function of abduction. The latter is viewed by Schurz as stimulating the formulation of new research questions and as "*crucial* ...The essential function of abductions is their role as *search* strategies which tell us which explanatory strategy conjecture we should set out *first* to further inquiry" (2008, 203–204).[31] The latter function consists in the justification of the conclusion, conditional to the justification of the premises; in the case of abduction this function is minor.

Based on such combination of characterization and differentiation of functions of abduction, Schurz classifies abduction along the following three dimensions: (i) the kind of hypothesis which is abduced; (ii) the kind of evidence the abduction should explain, and (iii) the cognitive mechanisms driving abduction.

According to Schurz, there are four types of abduction. First, abductions falling under the so-called *factual* type of abduction. These abductions are driven by known laws going from causes to effects, while both the evidence and abduced hypothesis are singular facts. The structure of these abductions can be schematically represented as follows (2008, 206):

Known Law: If Cx, then Ex
Known Evidence: Ea has occurred
= =
Abduced Conjecture: Ca could be the reason

Second, abductions falling under the so-called *law-abduction* type. These are driven either by pregiven scientific theories and/or by procedures aiming at unification of scientific theories. They can be, according to Schurz, creative in the sense that the operations involved in them construct something new, for example, a new theoretical model or even yield new theoretical concepts. The structure of these abductions is as follows (2008, 211):

---

31 Schurz draws here on (Hintikka 1998).

Background Law:	∀x(Cx → Ex)	Whatever contains sugar tastes sweet
Empirical Law to be Explained:	∀x(Fx → Ex)	All pineapples taste sweet

= =

Abduced Conjecture:	∀x(Fx → Cx)	All pineapples contain sugar

Third, abductions falling under the so-called *theoretical-model abduction* type. Here the explanandum should be an empirical law referring to a phenomenon and the abduction is driven by a pregiven scientific theory usually stated in a quantitative form. The task of abduction here is to find and state in a theoretical form the conditions describing the causes of the phenomenon which is thus restated in a theoretical-cum-quantitative form.

Worth noting are the following three claims made by Schurz (2003, 214, 216):

[1.] While for all other kinds of abduction [given above] we can provide a *general* formal pattern and algorithm by which one can *generate* a most promising explanatory hypothesis; we cannot provide such a general pattern for theoretical-model abduction because here all depends on *what theory* we are in.

[2.] [In abductions falling under the theoretical-model abduction type] the explanandum is ... given and the particular explanatory premises have to be found in the framework of the given theory.

[3.] What all abduction schemata discussed so far have in common is that they are driven by known laws or theories, and hence they work within a *given conceptual space*. In other words, the abduction schemata discussed so far cannot introduce *new concepts*.

Finally, Schurz turns to the so-called *second-order existential abduction type*; for the abductions falling under it holds that their "explanans postulates the existence of a new kind of property or relation" (2008, 216).

The explanans in abductions falling under this type consists of one or several general empirical phenomena or laws. What one abduces in them should be at least partly new – a new property or kind concept – governed by theoretical law which is at least partly epistemically new.

Schurz then divides this type into three subtypes – micropart, analogical, and hypothetical (common) cause – depending on what drives the abduction: extrapolation of known laws from the macro-level to the micro-level, or analogy, or attempts at unification. Among them, he views the third type as the "most fundamental kind of conceptually creative abduction" (2008, 218).

I shall not deal here with these subtypes for two reasons. First, they are based exclusively on examples from natural sciences and as central appears here the supposition that it is possible to state and employ scientific laws. Thus, one could raise some doubts about the applicability of Schurz's treatment of abduction to inferences performed in the grounded type of theory which, so as being inspired by symbolic interactionism, is a social-science-type of theory *par excellence*.

Second, and unrelated to the first reason, his paper (2008) approaches reasoning exclusively from the point of view of inference of a conclusion from certain premises. However, this approach, against which one cannot raise any objection given the fact that the subjected-matter of this paper is abduction, obscures the fact that reasoning involves in addition to inferences centered on arguments, other elements, for example, definitions. On the latter I will focus now.

5.5 The moral and a way out – definitions

The moral to be drawn from my treatment of induction and abduction, which drew on the works of Bacon, Peirce, Aliseda, and Schurz, is that it fails (may be with the possible exemption of the latter's fourth type of induction; the latter being subject to the two limitations spelled out above) in the attempt to provide a reconstruction of the *central feature of the grounded type of theory, namely, the emergence of new categories and properties of categories from indices*.

Thus, from this moral follows the sobering conclusion that the hope vested by many grounded theorists into inductive and/or abductive inferences, namely, "to give their research a stable, reliable foundation tempered (*gehärtetet*) by logic… [a hope] for a *rule driven*, *reproducible* as well as *valid* production of new scientific knowledge" (Reichertz 2003, 9) which would safeguard the latter's "*logical* as well as *innovative* character" (2003, 11) was not fulfilled by the works of those individuals.

Accordingly, one is confronted with the following question. *Is it still possible to provide a methodological treatment which would reconstruct that central feature of the grounded type of theory while treating reasoning not as a procedure based on some type of argument?* In my view, the answer is yes; and in order to delineate my position, let me return to that feature again.

The generation of one and the same category from several, mutually different indicators is schematically represented in Figure 1 above and illustrated in Figure 2 by the movement from characteristics of a dying patient which are apparent to a nurse and/or learned by her to the category of social loss of a dying patient. For this movement and generation holds that the category and the indicators, on the basis of which it was introduced, *are not mutually related in any necessary way*.[32]

This means that *first* certain characteristics of the data are identified and only *then* they are viewed as the indicators on the basis of which, in a final step, a new category is introduced. In addition, only by an initially *conventional* decision to view certain characteristics of data as indicators for a certain category can the latter can be introduced at all.

Such a characterization of an uni-directional movement given in the pair indicators – categories I view as explicable and reconstructible by means of what methodology and logic labels as *definition*. I understand the latter as a type of sentence whose logical form can be expressed as "$Y =_{df} X$", where Y is the *definiendum* (the defined entity) X the *definiens* (the defining entity) and "$=_{df}$" is the sign for the definition equality.[33] This unidirectional movement can then be further characterized in such a way, that *an indicator fulfills in the definition the role of a definiens* while *the category introduced on the basis of this indicator has in it the status of a definiendum*.

The nature of the definitions which are at work in the uni-directional movement given in the pair indicators – categories can be further specified by delineating the following three characteristics symptomatic for this movement.

First, for each of the indicators holds – with respect to a category – that it *suffices* for the definition of this category. Second, no set of indicators on the basis of which a category was introduced is *immune against further extensions*. Third, there-

---

32 For an opposing view on this see (Kelle 1996).
33 Here I am indebted to (Zouhar 2014; 2015). For a methodological analysis of definitions see also (Bielik – Gahér – Zouhar 2010).

fore, *no final set of indicators is necessary for the definitional introduction of a category*. Fourth, therefore, the indicators on the basis of which a certain category was introduced by means of definitions are mutually interchangeable in these definitions. This characteristic I view as a methodological explication of Glaser's and Strauss' restatement (1967, 23) of what Lazarsfeld labeled as the *interchangeability of indicators*.[34]

These four characteristics of definitions relating indicators to a category enable to subsume them under a type of definition which I label as the *cluster type of definition*.[35] Worth noting here is that this type differs from the standard understanding of the nature of definitions, because for any indicator which is not necessary for defining a category holds – *according to this understanding* – that it cannot be employed in the definition of this category.

Despite the fact that the cluster type of definition by its properties deviates from the standard understanding of the

---

34 On this see (Lazarsfeld 1951; 1955; 1958; 1959a; 1959b; 1966), (Jeřábek 2006) and (Schenk 2003). This restatement is based on grounded type of theory's view on the pair indicator-category which differs from Lazarsfeld's view on it. The principal difference from the point of view of methodology between these views is that while Lazarsfeld's focus is on the translation of a pregiven category into empirical indices, grounded type of theory's focus is on the generation of categories from indices.

35 Here I found very helpful the so-called *cluster concepts* going back to (Gasking 1960) and characterized as follows: "While it is possible to list sufficient conditions for the applicability of a cluster concept term, it is not possible to list any necessary conditions for its applicability. The reason ... for the impossibility of listing necessary conditions is that cluster concept terms have no definitions ... which make reference to the properties necessary for a term to be applied" (Cooper 1972, 496).

nature of definitions, I will now – as the conclusion of my study and as a test of fruitfulness of my delineation of this type – try to show that on the basis of this delineation it is possible to understand in a novel manner the difference between the so-called *quantitative* and the so-called *qualitative* approaches in sociology without viewing these approaches as being mutually inherently opposed and irreconcilable.

6. Beyond the Quantitative-Qualitative Divide: From Category to Magnitude

In the concluding part of my study I try to resolve the dispute between the representatives of the so-called qualitative and quantitative approaches sociology.

The opposition between the qualitative and quantitative approaches in sociology was succinctly characterized by E. G. Guba as follows: "The one precludes the other just as surely as belief in a round world precludes believing in a flat one" (1987, 31).

J. Morse delineated this opposition as follows (1995, 148):

> The *quantity* of data in a category is not theoretically important to the process of saturation. Richness of data is derived from detailed description, not the number of times something is stated. Frequency counts are out ... Further it is this process that is the most confusing to new investigators, because in quantitative methods the signification of numbers is carefully taught, and statistical significance is based on frequencies, averages, and the distribution of data. *Frequency* is central to the analysis, and if a particular instance is too abhorrent, it may be even deleted from the data as an "outlier" or an error. On the other hand, in qualitative analysis, the converse is true. It is often the infrequent gem that puts other data into perspective, that becomes the central key to understanding the data and for developing the model.

Charmaz also views the qualitative and quantitative approaches as mutually opposed and delineates this opposition by relating to the philosophy of positivism and by putting it into the context of philosophical categories *causal explanation* and *quantifiable variable*. She states (2006, pp. 4–5):

What kinds of methodological assumptions supported the move toward quantification? ...Beliefs in a unitary method of systematic observation, replicable experiments, operational definitions of concepts, logically deduced hypotheses, and confirmed evidence—often taken as *the* scientific method—formed the assumptions upholding quantitative methods. These assumptions supported positivism, the dominant paradigm of inquiry in routine natural science ... Social researchers who adopted the positivist paradigm aimed to discover causal explanations and to make predictions about an external, knowable world. Their beliefs in scientific logic, a unitary method, objectivity, and truth legitimized reducing qualities of human experience to quantifiable variables.

From the point of view of an attempt to overcome the declared opposition of qualitative and quantitative methods the phrase "quantifiable variable" appears to play a central role and this requires, first, to look at how both the *opponents* as well *proponents* of applicability of quantitative methods understand this term. As such an opponent I choose Blumer's views in (1956), stated in the framework of symbolic interactionism, on the entity he labels as "variable," and as such a proponent I choose Popper's views presented in the *Poverty of Historicism* (1957). I start with the former.

Blumer's aim in (1956) is to analyze the scheme which is employed in sociology with the aim to reduce the description of human group life to variables and their relations. This scheme he labels as "variable analysis," and views it as being employed in sociology understood as a (presumed) part of empirical science. The latter he characterizes by means of its aim, namely, (1954, 3)

to develop analytical schemes of the empirical world with which the given science is concerned. This is done by conceiving the world abstractly, that is in terms of classes of objects and of relations between such classes. Theoretical schemes are essentially proposals as to the nature of such classes and of their relations.

Against the employment of variable analysis in such a way understood sociology he states three arguments; two of them are relevant for this part of my study.[36]

First, in the sociology understood in such a way one lacks rules, guides, limitations and prohibitions which would govern the choice of variables. So, for example, stating the rule (1956, 683)

> that variables should be quantitative does not help, because with ingenuity one can impart a quantitative dimension to almost any qualitative item. One can usually construct some kind of measure or index of it … The proper insistence that a variable have a quantitative dimension does little to lessen the range of variety of items that may be set up as variables.

Second, sociology, in the sense of an empirical science, lacks the so-called *generic variables*, that is, variables that stand for abstract categories. In sociology-cum-empirical science there are three kinds of variables, namely, (1) historically/culturally specific categories, (ii) a special set of abstract categories, and (iii) a special set of class terms. Blumer claims that none of them really is a generic variable.

Historically/culturally specific categories (e.g., factory unemployment), that is, variables bound to a certain historical context do not stand "for items of abstract group life; their application to human groups around the world, to human groups in the past, and to conceivable human groups in the future is definitely restricted" (1956, 684). But even if the employment of these specific categories enables one to obtain propositions valid for certain specific historical/cultural

---

36 On the third argument see (Hanzel 2011).

settings, still – according to Blumer – "they do not yield the abstract knowledge that is the core of an empirical science" (1956, 684).

There exists, according to Blumer, a *special set of variables* which can be viewed without any doubt as abstract sociological categories (e.g., social cohesion, social integration, etc.), but the problem symptomatic for them is that they lack fixed or uniform indicators. Indicators assigned to them are such that they correspond to particular circumstances in which they are employed by a sociologist. Stated otherwise, these (1956, 684):

> indicators are tailored and used to meet the peculiar character of the local problem under study ... the abstract categories used as variables ... turn out with rare exceptions to be something other than generic categories. They are localized in terms of their content ... the use of such abstract categories in variable research adds little to generic knowledge of them.

Finally, class terms like "sex distribution" and "birth rate" hold universally for all human groups. But still, they cannot function in sociology as generic variables because, according to Blumer, their content is given by the particular instance of their application (e.g., "birth rate in Ceylon" and "sex distribution in Nebraska"). As a consequence, the relations which are found to hold between such particularized variables are localized and of a non-generic nature.

The conclusion that Blumer draws with respect to these three kinds of seemingly generic variables is that they are "predominantly disparate and localized in nature. Rarely do they refer satisfactorily to a dimension or property of abstract group life. With little exception they are bound temporally, spatially, and culturally, and are inadequately cast to serve as clear instances of generic sociological categories" (1956, 685).

Let me now turn to what Popper declares, with respect to the opposition between quantitative methods (he views employed in physics) and qualitative methods (he views as employed in sociology), about the employment of variables. In Chapter 9 of *Poverty of Historicism* he states the following (1957, 24):

> The social sciences know nothing that can be compared to the *mathematically formulated causal laws of physics*. Consider, for instance, the physical law that (for light of any given wave-length) the smaller the aperture through which a light ray passes, the greater is the angle of diffraction. A physical law of this type has the form: 'Under certain conditions, if magnitude A varies in a certain manner, then magnitude B also varies in some predictable manner'. In other words, such a law expresses a dependence of one quantity on another and the manner in which the one quantity depends on the other is laid down in exact quantitative terms. Physics has been successful in expressing all its laws in this form. In order to achieve this, its first task was to translate all physical qualities into quantitative terms. For instance, it had to replace the qualitative description of a certain kind of light—e.g. a bright yellow-greenish light—by a quantitative description: light of a certain wave-length and of a certain intensity. Such a process of quantitatively describing physical qualities is obviously a necessary pre-requisite for the quantitative formulation of causal physical laws.

By comparing the view of Blumer on what he labels as "variable" with Popper's view on what he labels as "magnitude" and synonymously as "quantity," it is obvious that *both hold to the putting into opposition of quantitative and qualitative methods in empirical science*. In what they differ is, of course, that while Popper (at least as it seems to me from that quote) views physics as methodologically superior (more advanced) as compared to sociology, because the former, but not the latter, gave up qualitative methods and started to employ quantitative methods, according to Blumer sociology is not less developed than other empirical science, but simply *different*; it does not employ the scheme labeled by him as "variable analysis."

What is behind their shared view about the opposition of quantitative and qualitative methods in empirical science is a shared understanding of the triple of terms "magnitude," "quantity" and "variable" which they both view as synonymous. This is explicitly seen when one turns to Popper's claim where he uses synonymously "magnitude" and "quantity," and where both should stand for an entity which varies, that is, for what is labeled by Blumer's "variable."

In my view, however, these three terms should not be viewed as synonymous. In order to differentiate them, I assign, utilizing (Berka 1983), to the term "magnitude" the following meaning: a conceptual entity unifying both a *qualitative* and a *qualitative* feature.

Berka's differentiation between these two aspects, seen by him as unified in magnitudes stated in empirical science, draws its inspiration partially on the attempt to disambiguate the meaning of the German term "Größe" which refers either to the *type* of magnitude (e.g., mass, length, GDP, etc.) or to the *values* of a type of a magnitude, that is, in the terminology introduced above to a *quantity*. This ambiguity then leads in German to the linguistic pun "Größe einer Größe." Based on that differentiation, Berka employed for the quantitative aspect of a magnitude the English term "size" and for the unity of a qualitative aspect and of a quantitative aspect the English term "magnitude." This differentiation then enables one to escape that German linguistic pun; its English translation being "size of a magnitude" and which differs from the standardly used expression "magnitude of a quantity."[37]

Based on such a characterization of magnitudes given in empirical science, one can differentiate between two types of variation, since they should always be dealt with separately both in empirical science and at the level metascientific-cum-methodological reflections. Expressions of the type "change of a variable," even if permissible in mathematics, should not be used in empirical science. Their employment in the latter is symptomatic for a lack of that differentiation.

First, when the researcher reflects on changes of a magnitude in the sense of a change of its *qualitative* aspect. For example, if a quantity would be assigned to the category labeled as "social loss of a patient dying in hospital," thus turning it into a magnitude, then the latter could not be applied in a sociological treatment of cases when patients are dying at home. Second, when the researcher reflects on changes of a magnitude in the sense of a change (variation) of its *quantitative* aspect, or, using Berka's terminology, of its size; she presupposes its qualitative aspect as given.

Based on these clarifications I can state several objections to the views of both Blumer and Popper presented above. As to the former, at least the following two objections are worth mentioning.

First, Blumer reduces magnitudes to their quantitative aspect and, as consequence of this reduction uses the term "variable" instead of the term "magnitude." There exists, however an important difference between variable and magnitude employed in empirical science, namely, that while the former acquires value from a set of *pure numbers* (e.g., 1, 2,

---

37 This expression is employed in methodological treatment of measurement in (Ellis 1960).

etc.), the latter from the set of denominated (impure) numbers (1 kilogram, 2 kilograms, etc.).[38]

Second, that reduction of magnitudes to their quantitative aspect on Blumer's part involves a complete neglect of their qualitative aspect. This then leads him to a completely distorted view on what he labels as "generic variable" or "abstract category." The fact that a magnitude involves a qualitative aspect sets a principal limitation on the applicability of propositions involving this magnitude to the state of affairs in the real (natural and/or social) world. Once such propositions, due to the lack of reference of the qualitative aspect of this magnitude, do not have a truth-maker in that world, then this magnitude cannot be applied for the development of an analytical scheme which would fit it.[39] This holds, contrary to the claim of Blumer, *to all empirical, that is, both to natural and social sciences*.

So, when he views the sociological terms as "social cohesion," "social integration," "sex" and "birth rate" as referring to unquestionably abstract sociological categories since "they can be applied universally to human group life; each has the same clear and common meaning in its application" (1956, 684), he misses a crucial point, namely, that he refers here to *human* group life and not to non-human life (e.g., of a group of termites living in a mount). In fact, one need not make a shift from group life of humans to that of termites to see, using Blumer's terminology, the *non-generic* nature of sociological categories. So, for example, it remains an open question, to groups of which species in the homo-lines of evolution, in addition to groups from the species *Homo*

---

38 This differentiation goes back to (Helmholtz 1930). On this see also (Hölder 1996).

39 I owe the term "truth-maker" to (Tooley 1977).

sapiens sapiens, can categories like "cohesion" and "social integration" be at all applied.

Based on this critique of Blumer, I label the *qualitative aspect of a magnitude as "category."*

Let me now turn the quote from Popper's *Poverty of Historicism*, given earlier. If one accepts the differentiation between the quantitative and qualitative aspect of a magnitude, then one can claim that Popper's reduction of *magnitudes* of physics to their *quantitative* aspect leads him, as consequence, to reflections on the variations of their quantitative aspect while simultaneously leaving out that they are applied to qualitatively specific entities. This is obvious from the example he uses in that quote. He describes the application of magnitudes like wave length and intensity to an entity with a specific quality, namely, light.

In fact, even if one does not accept such a differentiation, still one can identify a contradiction between Popper's claim about the purely quantitative nature of physics and his example from physics which he employs as an illustration of those reflections. Contrary to that claim, he refers in his example to two physical qualities assigned to light, namely, *intensity* and *wave length*, whose variations of sizes are placed into a relation stated in the framework of a scientific law.

For a better understanding of two of my central claims, namely, that a *magnitude unifies a qualitative and a quantitative aspect* and that the *former has the status of a category*, I shall try to illustrate them by utilizing the sequence of three definitions stated by Newton in the *Principia*.

Definition V states the following: "*Centripetal force is the force by which bodies are drawn from all sides, are impelled or in any way tend, toward some point as to a center*" (1999, 404).

In my view, what Newton defines here is the centripetality of a force by means of an effect of it, namely, that it draws all bodies from all sides, impels them or let them tend in any way, to some point as a center. This definition may thus be restated as follows:

Centripetal force $=_{df}$ *It draws all bodies from all sides, impels them or let them tend in any way, to some point as a center.*

Accordingly, I interpret the statement "*It draws all bodies from all sides, impels them or let them tend in any way, to some point as a center*" as referring to an *indicator* which is given in the definiens, while the expression "centriptal force" has, with respect to this indicator, the status of a *category of physics* given in the definiendum. And I view both this indicator and this category as understood in this definition in a *purely qualitative manner*.

With respect to this, worth stating are Definitions VII and VIII (1999, 407):[40]

> *The accelerative quantity of centripetal force is the measure of this force that is proportional to the velocity which it generates in a given time.*

---

40 I leave out Definition VI running as follows: "*The absolute quantity of centripetal force is the measure of this force that is greater or less in proportion to the efficacy of the cause propagating it from a center through the surrounding regions*" (1999, 406). I do not deal with it because Newton does not assign in it any quantity to the centripetal force; the reason for this being that he assigns no quantity to the cause to which he refers here. With respect to the force of gravity he assigns a quantity only in Book III, where he proves that the quantity of mass of a central body from which emanates the force of gravity as a kind of centripetal force, determines the quantity (size) of efficacy of this kind force, and where under this efficacy he understands acceleration of a body subjected to this kind of force.

The motive quantity of centripetal force is the measure of this force that is proportional to the motion which it generates in a given time.

In the definiens of each of them, the indicator-effect of the centripetal force (delineated as a quality by the definiens of Definition V) is assigned a quantity: in Definition VII it is the change (variation) of speed in a fixed interval of time, in Definition VIII it is the change (variation) of motion in a fixed interval of time. By these two assignments the definiens-indicator from Definition V turns into two different magnitudes. Their difference is given by their quantitative aspect; they are identical as to the quality/category they share – the effect of a centripetal force described in Definition V as the drawing of bodies from all sides, impelling them or let them tend in any way, to some point as a center.

In the *definienda* of both definitions, the category labeled in Definition V as "centripetal force" (and understood there as a quality) turns into two different magnitudes. Their difference is given by the difference of their respective quantities proportional to the quantities computed in their respective *definiensia*; their identity is given by the fact that they share the same category/quality – it is a centripetal force.

If one now compares Newton's movement from the definiens to the definiendum in those three definitions, as well as his movement from Definition V to Definitions VII and VIII, with the movement from indices to categories given in the grounded type of theory, one discovers the following.

First, what Newton's move from the definiens to the definiendum in Definition V shares with the movement from indices to a category as given in the grounded type of theory is the fact that in both one deals only with qualities. There exists, however, an important difference between them. While in the grounded type of theory several different indicators –

leading to one and the same category – should be applied, in Newton's Definition V only one indicator is considered as a definiens. It remains an open question if in the framework of physics some additional indicators could be employed in the definition of the centripetality of a force.

Second, Newton's movement from Definition V to that of VII and VII as well the move from the definiens to definiendum in Definitions VII and VIII, respectively, has no counterpart in the grounded type of theory because the latter *lacks an assigning of respective quantities to both indices and categories.*

Ultimately, I am led to the following conclusion. *The grounded type of theory is a qualitative type of theory because it refrains from the move in which categories and their indices would be complemented by their respective quantities and where this move would turn both into magnitudes. In this sense the grounded type of theory cannot be viewed as being inherently opposed to, but only as different from those (natural-science and social-science) theories in the framework of which this move has already been accomplished.*

This conclusion can, in turn, be viewed as a deeper justification as well as explanation of Strauss' and Corbin's delineation of the qualitative direction in sociological research which I quoted at the beginning of this study. The fact that in this type of research "mathematical techniques are eschewed or are of minimal use" (Strauss 1987, 2) and their "findings [are] not arrived at by means of statistical procedures or other means of quantification" (Strauss – Corbin 1990, 17) indicates that the categories and indices in that research are not complemented by their respective quantities. If such complementation would exist, then mathematical procedures (e.g., statistical procedures) could and should have been applied to them.

References

Aliseda, A. (2003): Mathematical reasoning vs. abductive reasoning. *Synthese* 134 (1–2): 25–44.

Ajdukiewicz, K. (1955): Franciszek Bacon z Werulamu. In: Bacon 1955: VII–XCVIII.

Anderson, D. R. (1986): The evolution of Peirce's concept of abduction. *Transactions of the Charles S Peirce Society* 22 (2): 145–166.

Bacon, F. (1955): *Novum Organum*. Warszawa: PWN.

Bacon, F. (2003): *New Organon*. Cambridge: Cambridge University Press.

Barker, S. F. (1957): *Induction and Hypothesis*. Ithaca (NY): Cornell University Press.

Berka, K. (1983): *Measurement*. Dordrecht: Reidel.

Bielik, L. – Gahér, F. – Zouhar, M. (2010): O definíciách a definovaní. *Filozofia* 65 (8): 719–737.

Blumer, H. (1954): What is wrong with social theory? *American Sociological Review* 19 (1): 3–10.

Blumer, H. (1956): Sociological analysis and the "variable." *American Sociological Review* 21 (6): 683–690.

Brewka, G. (1991): *Nonmonotonic Reasoning*. Cambridge: Cambridge University Press.

Burks, A. W. (1946): Peirce's theory of abduction. *Philosophy of Science* 13 (4): 301–306.

Carnap, R. (1950): *Logical Foundations of Probability*. Cambridge (MA): Harvard University Press.

Carnap, R. (1952): *The Continuum of Inductive Methods*. Cambridge (MA): Harvard University Press.

Charmaz, K. (1983): The grounded theory method. In: Emerson, R. M. (Eds.): *Contemporary Field Research*. Boston (MA), Little Brown: 109–126.

Charmaz, K. (2006): *Constructing Grounded Theory*. London: SAGE.

Cheng, C.-Y. (1969): *Peirce's and Lewis' Theories of Induction*. The Hague: M. Nijhoff.

Cmorej, P. (2000): Úvod do problematiky metodológie vied (III) [Introduction to the poblems of methodology of science (III)]. *Organon F* 7 (3): 326–337.

Cooper, D. E. (1972): Definitions and 'clusters'. *Mind* 81 (324): 495–503.

Davis, F. (1961): Deviance disavowal. *Social Problems* 9: 120–129.

Dey, I. (1999): *Grounding Grounded Theory*. San Diego (CA): Academic Press.

Ellis, B. (1960): Fundamental problems of basic measurement. *Australasian Journal of Philosophy* 38 (1): 37–47.

Filkorn V. (1974): Baconov indukcionizmus [Bacon's inductivism]. *Filozofia* 29 (3): 215–229.

Flores, A. J. (2014): Peirce's theory of the origin of abduction in Aristotle. *Transactions of the Charles S Peirce Society* 50 (2): 252–280.

Fritz, C. A. (1960): What is induction? *Journal of Philosophy* 57 (4): 126–138.

Gasking, D. (1960): Clusters. *Australasian Journal of Philosophy* 38 (1): 1–36.

Glaser, B. G. (1978): *Theoretical Sensitivity*. Mill Valley (CA): The Sociology Press.

Glaser, B. G. (1992): *Basics of Grounded Theory Analysis*. Mill Valley (CA): The Sociology Press.

Glaser, B. G. (1998): *Doing Grounded Theory*. Mill Valley (CA): The Sociology Press.

Glaser, B. G. (2005): *The Grounded Theory Perspective III*. Mill Valley (CA): The Sociology Press.

Glaser, B. G. – Strauss, A. L. (1964a): Awareness contexts and social interaction. *American Sociological Review* 29 (5): 669–679.

Glaser, B. G. – Strauss, A. L. (1964b): The social loss of a dying patient. *American Journal of Nursing* 64 (6): 119–121.

Glaser, B. G. – Strauss, A. L. (1965a): Discovery of substantive theory. *American Behavioral Scientist* 8 (6): 5–12.

Glaser, B. G. – Strauss, A. L. (1965b): *Awareness of Dying*. Chicago: Aldine.

Glaser, B. G. – Strauss, A. L. (1967): *The Discovery of Grounded Theory*. Chicago: Aldine.

Guba, E. G. (1987): What we have learned about naturalistic evaluation? *Evaluation Practice* 8 (1): 23–43.

Helmholtz, H. H. von (1930): *Counting and Measuring*. New York: Van Nostrand.

Hanzel, I. (2011): Beyond Blumer and symbolic interactionism. *Philosophy of Social Sciences* 41 (3): 303–326.

Hendricks, V. F. – Faye, J. (1999): Abducting explanation. In Magnani, L. – Nersessian, N. – Thagard, P. (Eds.): *Model-Based Reasoning in Scientific Discovery*. Dordrecht, Kluwer: 271–292.

Hilpinen, R. (2000): Aristotelian syllogistic as foundation of C. S. Peirce's theory of reasoning. In Sfendoni-Mentzou, D. (Ed.): *Aristotle and Contemporary Science*, Vol. I. New York, Peter Lang: 109–125.

Hintikka, J. (1998): What is abduction? *Transactions of the Charles S Peirce Society* 34 (3): 503–533.

Hölder, O. (1996): The Axioms of quantity and the theory of measurement, I. *Journal of Mathematical Psychology* 40 (3): 237–252.

Holton, J. (2007): The coding process and its challenges. In: Bryant, A. – Charmaz, K. (Eds.): *The SAGE Book of Grounded Theory*. London, SAGE: 237–261.

Horton, M. (1973): In defence of Francis Bacon. *Studies in the History and Philosophy of Science A* 4 (3): 241–278.

Jeon, Y.-H. (2004): The application of grounded theory and symbolic interactionism. *Scandinavian Journal of Caring Science* 18 (3): 249–256.

Jeřábek, H. (2006): *Paul Felix Lazarsfeld's Research Methodology*. Prague: Carolinum Press.

John, R. (1980): Theory construction in sociology. *Mid-American Review of Sociology* V (1): 15–36.

Kelle, U. (1990): Theories as heuristic tools in qualitative research. In: Maso, I. (Ed.): *Openness in Research*. Assen, Van Gorcum: 33–50.

Kelle, U. (1994): *Empirisch begründete Theoriebildung*. Weinheim: Deutsches Studien Verlag.

Kelle, U. (1996): Die Bedeutung theoretischen Vorwissens in der Methodologie der Grounded Theory. In: Strobe, R. – Böttiger, A. (Hg.): *Wahre Geschichten?* Baden Baden, Nomos Verlag: 23–47.

Kempski, J. von (1992a): Charles Sanders Peirce und die Apagoge des Aristoteles. In Kempski 1992b: 310–319.

Kempski, J. von (1992b): *Schriften*, Bd. 3. Frankfurt am Main: Suhrkamp.

Keynes, J. M. (1921): *A Treatise on Probability*. London: MacMillan and Co.

Lazarsfeld, P. F. (1951): Qualitative measurement in social sciences. In: Lerner, D. – Lasswell, H. D. (Eds.): *The Policy Sciences*. Stanford, Stanford University Press: 155–192.

Lazarsfeld, P. F. (1955): Interpretations of statistical relations as a research operation. In: Lazarsfeld, P. F. – Rosenberg, M. (Eds.): *The Language of Social Research*. New York, The Free Press: 115–124.

Lazarsfeld, P. F. (1958): Evidence and inference in social research. *Daedalos* 87: 99–130.

Lazarsfeld, P. F. (1959a): Problems in methodology. In: Merton, R. K. – Broom, L. – Coltrell, L. S. (Eds.): *Sociology Today*. New York, Basic Books: 39–78.

Lazarsfeld, P. F. (1959b): Methodological problems in empirical social research. In: *Transactions of the Fourth World Congress of Sociology*, Volume II. London, International Sociological Association: 225–249.

Lazarsfeld, P. F. (1962): The sociology of empirical research. *American Sociological Review* 27 (6): 757–767.

Lazarsfeld, P. F. (1966): Concept formation and measurement in the behavioral sciences. In: Direnzo, G. J. (Ed.): *Concepts, Theory and Explanations in the Behavioral Sciences*. New York, Random House: 144–202.

Levi, I. (1996): *For the Sake of Argument*. Cambridge: Cambridge University Press.

Mey, G. – Mruck, K. (2007): Methodology. *Historical Social Research*, Supplement 19: 11–39.

Mill, J. S. (1974): *A System of Logic*. London: Routledge and Kegan Paul.

Morse, J. M. (1991): Strategies for sampling. In: Morse, J. M. (Ed.): *Qualitative Nursing Research*. New York, SAGE: 127–145.

Morse, J. M. (1995): The significance of saturation. *Qualitative Health Research* 5 (2): 147–149.

Newton, I. (1999): *The Principia*. Berkeley: University of California Press.

Peirce, C. S. (1960–1966): *Collected Papers*, Vol. 1.–7. Cambridge (MA): Belknap Press of Harvard University Press.

Peirce, C. S. (1975): *The New Elements of Mathematics*, Vol. IV. The Hague: Mouton.

Popper, K. R. (1957): *Poverty of Historicism*. Boston: Beacon Press.

Psillos, S. (2011): An explorer upon untrodden ground. In: Gabbay, D. M. – Hartman, S. – Woods, J. (eds.) (2011): *Inductive Logic*. Amsterdam, North Holland: 117–152.

Reichenbach, H. (1949): *Theory of Probability*. Berkeley: University of California Press.

Reichertz, J. (2003): *Die Abduktion in der qualitativen Sozialforschung*. Opladen: Leske und Budrich.

Riemer, I. (1988): *Konzeption und Begründung der Induktion*. Würzburg: Königshausen und Neumann.

Salmon, W. C. (1966): *Foundations of Scientific Inference*. Pittsburgh: University of Pittsburgh Press.

Schenk, J. (2003): K hlavným princípom Lazarsfeldovej koncepcie metodológie [On the main principles of Lazarsfeld's conception of methodology]. In Schenk, J. a kolektív: *Paul Felix Lazarsfeld*. Bratislava, SOFA: 15–52.

Schurz, G. (2008): Patterns of abduction. *Synthese* 164 (2): 201–234.

Strauss, A. L. (1970): Discovering new theory from previous theory. In: Shibutani, T. (Ed.): *Human Nature and Collective Behavior*. Englewood Cliffs (NJ), Prentice Hall: 46–53.

Strauss, A. L. (1978): A social world perspective. *Studies in Symbolic Interaction* 1: 119–128.

Strauss, A. L. (1984): Social worlds and segmentation process. *Studies in Symbolic Interaction* 5: 123–139.

Strauss, A. L. (1987): *Qualitative Analysis for Social Scientists*. Cambridge: Cambridge University Press.

Strauss, A. L. – Corbin, J. (1990): *Basics of Qualitative Research*. New Bury Park: SAGE.

Strübing, J. (2007): Research as pragmatic problem solving. In: Bryant, A. – Charmaz, K. (Eds.): *The SAGE Book of Grounded Theory*. London, SAGE: 581–601.

Tooley, M. (1977): The nature of laws. *Canadian Journal of Philosophy* 7 (4): 667–698.

Truschkat, I. – Kaiser-Belz, M. – Reinartz, V. (2007): Grounded Theory in Qualifikationsarbeiten. *Historical Social Research*, Supplement 19: 232–257.

Viceník, J. (2001): Úvod do problematiky metodológie vied (V) [Introduction to the problems of methodology of science (V)]. *Organon F* 8 (1): 91–103.

Walker, H. A. – Cohen, B. P. (1985): Scope statements. *American Sociological Review* 50 (3): 288–301.

Zouhar, M. (2014): Klasifikácia definícií [Classification of definitions]. *Teorie vědy* 36 (3): 337–358.

Zouhar, M. (2015): Logická forma definícií [The logical form of definitions]. *Filozofia* 70 (3): 161–174.